Shelves and Bookcases

PRO TIPS AND SIMPLE STEPS

Meredith® Books
Des Moines, Iowa

Stanley® Books
An imprint of Meredith® Books

Stanley Shelves & Bookcases
Editor: Ken Sidey
Writer: Peter J. Stephano
Project Designer: James E. Boelling
Consulting craftsman: Bernard Von Ruden
Senior Associate Design Director: Tom Wegner
Assistant Editor: Harijs Priekulis
Copy Chief: Terri Fredrickson
Copy and Production Editor: Victoria Forlini
Editorial Operations Manager: Karen Schirm
Managers, Book Production: Pam Kvitne,
    Marjorie J. Schenkelberg
Contributing Copy Editor: Kim Catanzarite
Technical Proofreaders: George Granseth, Griffin Wall
Technical Editor, The Stanley Works: Mike Maznio
Contributing Proofreaders: Chardel Blaine, Beth Lastine,
    Ellie Sweeney, James Stepp
Contributing Illustrator: ArtRep Services
Contributing Photographer: Scott Little
Indexer: Donald Glassman
Electronic Production Coordinator: Paula Forest
Editorial and Design Assistants: Renee E. McAtee,
    Karen McFadden

Additional Editorial Contributions from
    Image Studios
Account Executive: Lisa Egan
Photography: Bill Rein
Set Building: Rick Nadke

Production
Image I.T.
Production Manager: Jill Ellsworth
Account Rep: Cher King
Prepress Operator: Eric Abraham

Meredith® Books
Publisher and Editor in Chief: James D. Blume
Design Director: Matt Strelecki
Managing Editor: Gregory H. Kayko
Executive Editor, Gardening and Home Improvement:
    Benjamin W. Allen
Executive Editor, Home Improvement: Larry Erickson

Director, Operations: George A. Susral
Director, Production: Douglas M. Johnston

Vice President and General Manager: Douglas J. Guendel

Meredith Publishing Group
President, Publishing Group: Stephen M. Lacy
Vice President-Publishing Director: Bob Mate

Meredith Corporation
Chairman and Chief Executive Officer: William T. Kerr

Chairman of the Executive Committee: E.T. Meredith III

Thanks to
Woodcraft, West Des Moines

All of us at Stanley® Books are dedicated to providing you with
the information and ideas you need to enhance your home and
garden. We welcome your comments and suggestions about
this book. Write to us at:
    Meredith Corporation
    Stanley Books
    1716 Locust St.
    Des Moines, IA 50309–3023

If you would like more information on other Stanley products,
call 1-800-STANLEY or visit us at: www.stanleyworks.com
Stanley® and the notched rectangle around the Stanley name
are registered trademarks of The Stanley Works and
subsidiaries.

If you would like to purchase any of our home improvement,
cooking, crafts, gardening, or home decorating and design
books, check wherever quality books are sold. Or visit us at:
meredithbooks.com

Note to the Readers: Due to differing conditions, tools,
and individual skills, Meredith Corporation assumes no
responsibility for any damages, injuries suffered, or losses
incurred as a result of following the information published
in this book. Before beginning any project, review the
instructions carefully, and if any doubts or questions remain,
consult local experts or authorities. Because codes and
regulations vary greatly, you always should check with
authorities to ensure that your project complies with all
applicable local codes and regulations. Always read and
observe all of the safety precautions provided by
manufacturers of any tools, equipment, or supplies,
and follow all accepted safety procedures.

CONTENTS

PROJECTS TO MEET YOUR NEEDS

Few homes come equipped with adequate display or storage space. That's why bookcases and shelves top almost everyone's home furnishings list.

Ready-made pieces abound in the marketplace. The trouble is, if they're well-made, they're usually expensive. Or if they're low-cost, they're probably not sturdy and durable. Ready-to-assemble furniture presents another buyers' option, but it's difficult to find a bookcase or shelf that exactly meets your needs, your space, and your decor, and still fits your budget.

Building your own bookcase or shelving is the solution. And it isn't difficult to do. In fact, if you've done home repairs or some remodeling, you've likely developed some of the woodworking skills needed to build your own pieces. The rest will come as you begin building. Along the way, you'll gain confidence and enjoy learning a new craft. Even more, you'll feel the satisfaction of doing it yourself. Before you get started, though, some definitive planning is necessary.

Prime considerations

When you're thinking about adding bookcases or shelves, begin by asking the following questions:

■ What is the main purpose of the piece?
■ What will best meet that purpose, a bookcase or simple shelving? A quick-to-build, low-cost utility piece or one of furniture quality?
■ Where will it go?
■ What size and style do I want?
■ What material will work best?
■ Should it be painted or naturally finished?

Other factors also influence your final decision on what to build.

Work space: With a basement, garage, or spare room available as a workshop, you can build large projects. A smaller space limits you to smaller projects, or those that can be broken down into subassemblies or made with parts precut at the lumberyard or home center.

Do-it-yourself skills: If you're new to woodworking, start with simpler projects, then move on to larger, more involved ones. All the skills you need to build the projects in this book are presented in clear, step-by-step instructions. Stanley Pro Tips offer additional advice to help you work faster and easier. Above all, work safely. Use the right tool, in the right way, for the right job.

Budget: Buying tools for a project adds to its cost, but those additions to your workshop are an investment that can save time and money on future projects and repairs.

Time: It doesn't pay to rush. If you're pressed for time, build your projects in stages. The Prestart Checklist provided with each project gives you a clear idea of the time, as well as the skills, tools, and materials needed to complete it.

Learn new skills and feel the satisfaction of doing it yourself as you add new storage space for your home.

CHAPTER PREVIEW

Project gallery
page 6

Design standards
page 8

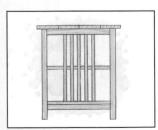

Customizing projects
page 9

There's nothing like having the satisfaction of building exactly what you need, exactly the way you want it to look. And with shelves and bookcases, it's not as difficult as you may think.

PROJECT GALLERY

To help you get started building your own projects, *Stanley Shelves and Bookcases* features eight projects designed specifically for this book, each with complete step-by-step instructions. Each project offers several options, enabling you to create a piece suited to your needs and style. For example, you'll find instructions on how to change the dimensions of a piece and how to add an appealing decorative treatment. Remember, too, that you have the option to change woods and finishes.

The chapter "Easy, Great-Looking Shelves to Build" shows you how to build a simple display shelf, a "floating" wall shelf, expandable utility shelving, stackable modular boxes, and a multipurpose stand. The chapter on bookcase projects shows how to build a fixed-shelf bookstand, a bookcase with adjustable shelves, and a library-style built-in bookcase with optional doors.

This simple wall-mounted shelf (page 64) can be trimmed or finished to fit any decor. It's a great first project to make if you are just getting started in woodworking.

Floating wall shelves (page 68) provide an attractive, sturdy stage for books, knickknacks, or collections. They're easy to build in a variety of custom-fit sizes.

Modular boxes (page 72) make great display or storage units for a child's room or anywhere in the home. Another plus is that they're low cost: You can make several boxes from one sheet of plywood.

This multipurpose oak stand, designed in popular Mission style (page 76), serves as a TV stand in a living room, a worktable in a home office, or attractive storage just about anywhere in the house.

An economical way to create sturdy utility shelving fast (page 84), these units can be built to the dimensions you need for garage, basement, laundry, or storage room.

This 30-inch-tall, fixed-shelf bookcase (page 92) is another good starter project for the beginning woodworker. The extended sides with handles are an easy option.

This 4-foot adjustable-shelf bookcase (page 98) is an all-purpose piece around the house. As with all the projects in this book, it can be painted or stained and finished to match any decor.

With the simple addition of molding, this 6-foot bookshelf resembles a built-in piece (page 106). Optional doors can be added at the bottom to provide concealed storage.

DESIGN STANDARDS

The greatest advantage to building something yourself is crafting it to best suit your needs or lifestyle. Few woodworkers can resist altering the plan they begin with! However, when it comes to shelves and bookcases, following a few basic design guidelines ensures that your piece will be not only functional, but good-looking as well.

If all books were the same size and shape, bookcase and shelf planning would be simple. But that's not the case. For attractiveness as well as stability, the size and spacing of shelves are dictated by what you'll put on them. Books vary greatly in size

(see below), and if you want to house entertainment equipment in the same unit, you'll need shelf depths from 18 to 20 inches (for most systems) and spacing between shelves customized to fit your stereo, speakers, and accessories.

Shelving units that accommodate both books and audiovisual equipment are often modular components. A deeper unit holds the large equipment, and side or top units provide book or display storage.

Know the no-sag limits

You also must consider the shelving material's span limit. That's how far an

unsupported shelf will span under load without sagging or breaking *(page 27)*. Solid hardwood boards of ¾-inch thickness, for instance, span a greater distance than particleboard of the same thickness.

Keep it within reach

Design shelves with their users in mind. As shown below, men generally have a greater maximum reach than women, and teens can reach higher than children. While that may seem obvious, building shelves that no one can access is a waste of time and materials. Likewise, shelves shouldn't be too low to be used easily.

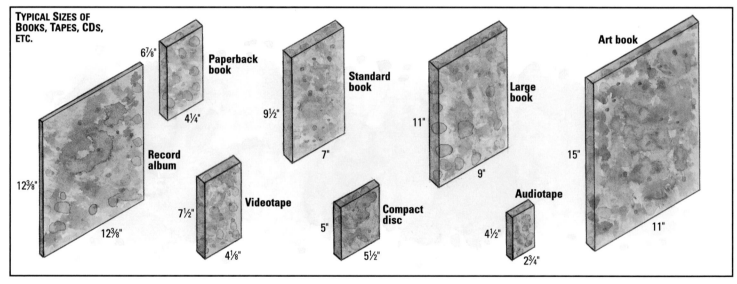

TYPICAL SIZES OF BOOKS, TAPES, CDS, ETC.

Paperback book — 6⅞", 4¼"
Standard book — 9½", 7"
Large book — 11", 9"
Art book — 15", 11"
Record album — 12⅜", 12⅜"
Videotape — 7½", 4⅛"
Compact disc — 5", 5½"
Audiotape — 4½", 2¾"

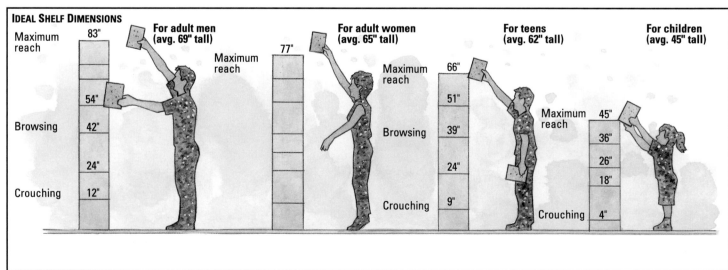

IDEAL SHELF DIMENSIONS

For adult men (avg. 69" tall) — Maximum reach 83", 54", Browsing 42", 24", Crouching 12"

For adult women (avg. 65" tall) — Maximum reach 77", Browsing 39", 24", Crouching 9"

For teens (avg. 62" tall) — Maximum reach 66", 51", 39", 24", Crouching 9"

For children (avg. 45" tall) — Maximum reach 45", 36", 26", 18", Crouching 4"

CUSTOMIZING PROJECTS

As you review the projects in this book, keep in mind that it's possible to change the dimensions of most of them. (The modular boxes, however, were designed to get the most from a 4×8 sheet of plywood.)

At the same time, changing the size of one component sometimes means a change in another. For example, if you create deeper shelves in a bookcase , you will also have to widen the sides of the unit. That means buying wider stock.

Making changes in height isn't usually a concern, unless the project plan includes a back. Then you'll need enough stock to accommodate the change. Carefully think through any changes and plan for what they'll entail. Draw and label your plans carefully. If possible, have an experienced woodworker check your plans and dimensions. You will also find help at your local lumberyard or home center.

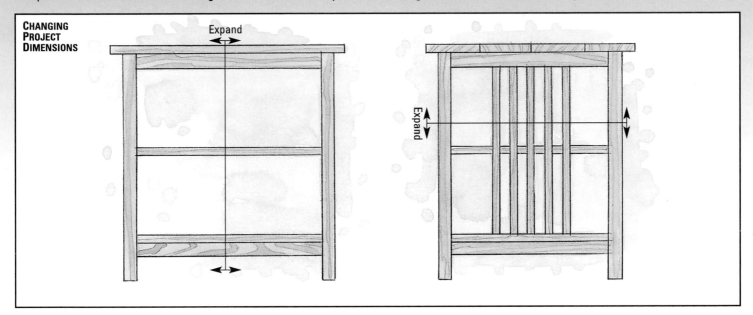

CHANGING PROJECT DIMENSIONS

Accessible to all

Special circumstances sometimes require altering or adapting standard dimensions. In a home designed for the elderly, for instance, the highest functional shelf should be lowered 3 inches from the standard 68 inches. The lowest drawer or shelf should be moved up 3 inches. A lower work surface or tabletop is in order too. It should be about 1½ inches lower than the normal 35 inches.

Those who are physically disabled and work from a wheelchair also have special needs. For them, a tabletop or work surface should be no higher than 31 inches from the floor. To accommodate a wheelchair under a table, a free space 30 inches wide by 29½ inches deep must be provided. This allows for 24 inches of forward reach. Shelf height should also be taken into consideration, with most frequently used items within reach. For more information on space allowances and reach ranges, write to the U.S. Department of Justice, 950 Pennsylvania Ave. NW, Disability Rights Section–NYAVE, Washington, DC 20530; or log on to the Americans with Disabilities Act (ADA) web site at www.usdoj.gov/crt/ada/.

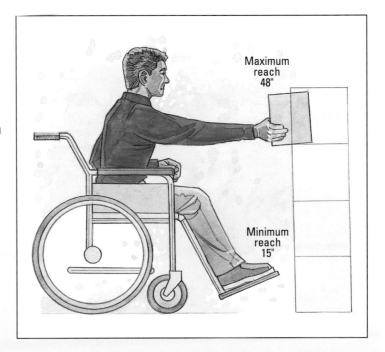

Maximum reach 48"

Minimum reach 15"

CHOOSING TOOLS

You don't need a workshop full of expensive tools to build top-quality bookcases and shelves. You can avoid the cost of some tools by having wood and sheet goods cut to size when you purchase them. Most lumberyards and home centers will cut or plane material for you. You'll pay extra for this service, but it's less expensive than buying a planer or table saw.

You probably already have some of the basic tools described on *pages 12 and 13*. Quality is important, though, so if you're starting your first serious woodworking project, you may need to upgrade. Each new project may call for the purchase of a specific tool. Budget that cost along with the materials and consider it an investment in future projects.

Shop smart

Many tool manufacturers produce two product lines: inexpensive "hobby" tools and more costly, heavier-duty tools for serious or professional use. Check out top-of-the-line tools and you'll quickly see the difference between them and the ones made cheaply. A good hammer, for instance, will have a drop-forged and heat-tempered steel head; the handle will be ash or hickory, or fiberglass; or it will be one-piece, all-steel construction.

The metal on all hand tools should be flawlessly machined; handles should be tight-fitting and hefty. When purchasing hand tools, buy the best you can afford, and consider the relatively few dollars more you've paid to be a lifetime investment in your satisfaction, safety, and productivity.

When shopping for power tools, on the other hand, don't buy more features than you need. Professional power tools can cost many times more than their hobbyist cousins. Capacity and durability are worth the money to professionals who use power tools all day, every day, but for most do-it-yourselfers, an 18-volt cordless drill can't do more than a 12-volt one.

Generally you can tell quality by "fit and finish." A well-made, neatly assembled housing usually reflects carefully made inner workings. Make sure cast steel or aluminum parts are smoothly milled, triggers and controls are user-friendly, and electrical cords are sturdy. Compare portable power tools by their amperage ratings rather than their horsepower; the higher the rating, the more power the tool delivers.

Buy the best hand tool you can afford—but no more power tool than you need.

CHAPTER PREVIEW

Basic tools
page 12

Power tools
page 14

Stationary power tools
page 16

Accessories
page 18

You don't need a warehouse full of the latest, most expensive tools to build shelves and bookcases. A few high-quality power tools and their accessories, such as the circular saw and layout square being used here to cut a shelf board at a precise 90-degree angle, will speed your work and ensure high-quality results.

SAFETY FIRST

Always wear eye and ear protection when working with power tools.

Use clamps to hold work materials securely to sawhorses, bench, or table.

BASIC TOOLS

These two pages display a collection of essential hand tools. You won't need all of them to begin woodworking, but you will find all of them useful by the time you've tackled several projects.

Tools for cutting and shaping
A **crosscut saw** cuts wood across the grain (rip saws have special teeth to cut with the grain). A **backsaw** creates a finer, more accurate cut and is typically used in conjunction with a **miter box** to cut accurate angles. The thin, narrow blade of a **coping saw** follows tight curves. Look for saws with solid wood handles, which are more comfortable and sturdy than hollow plastic ones. A **jack plane** smooths and squares the long sides of larger pieces of wood, while a **block plane** shaves their ends and angles. **Wood chisels** pare away material and cut recesses. A **rasp** and **Surform plane** quickly remove wood. When buying these cutting tools, look for precision machining. A sanding block holds sandpaper flat and firmly as you smooth wood. For trimming small pieces, a **utility knife** is handy.

Tools for joining wood pieces
A 7-ounce **finishing hammer** drives brads and small nails. A **nail set** pushes a nail head below the wood's surface. Use a **dead-blow hammer** to avoid marring wood. For setting screws, you'll need **phillips** and **standard screwdrivers** in several sizes.

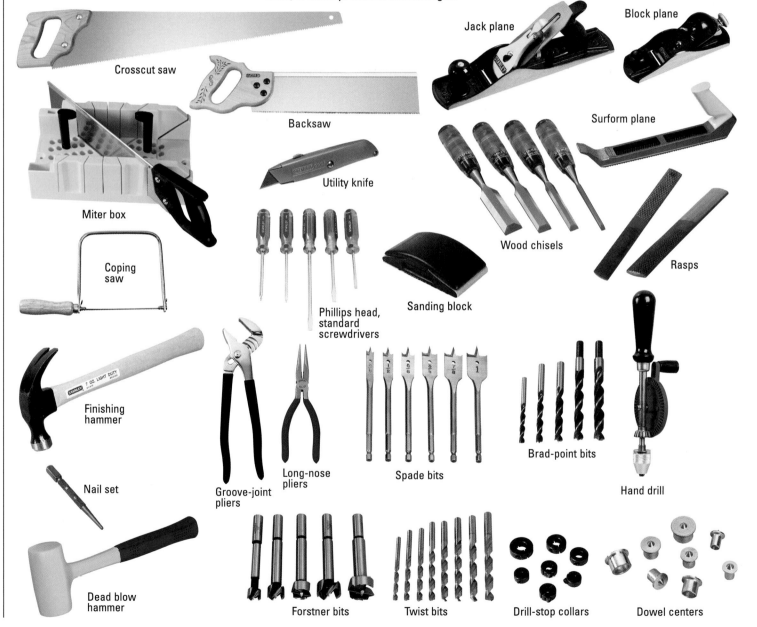

Crosscut saw

Backsaw

Jack plane

Block plane

Surform plane

Utility knife

Miter box

Wood chisels

Rasps

Coping saw

Phillips head, standard screwdrivers

Sanding block

Finishing hammer

Long-nose pliers

Spade bits

Brad-point bits

Hand drill

Nail set

Groove-joint pliers

Dead blow hammer

Forstner bits

Twist bits

Drill-stop collars

Dowel centers

Use a **hand drill** and **twist bits** or **brad-point bits** to make pilot holes for screws. Turn to **Forstner bits** for clean-sided, flat-bottomed holes or **spade bits** for rougher cut ones. **Drill-stop collars** control hole depth. **Dowel centers** help correctly align holes when making dowel joints.

C-clamps and adjustable **pipe clamps** or **bar clamps** hold work securely during gluing or machining. **Quick clamps** eliminate hand-turning to tighten. A **miter clamp** holds pieces at a precise 90-degree angle.

Tools for measuring and marking
A 12-foot **steel tape** is handy for making large measurements accurately and conveniently—the best have wide, thick, tempered-steel blades with large high-visibility numbering. A **framing square** is handy for checking right angles and laying out 90-degree lines—choose one on which the gradations are stamped into the metal, rather than simply painted on. A **layout square** quickly shows you a 45-degree angle or the square cutoff on a board.

A **combination square** does that, too, but it's blade length is adjustable. For checking small 90-degree angles, a **try square** fills the bill. To measure odd angles and transfer them for duplication, use a **sliding bevel**. Use a **marking gauge** to scribe long lines. A **divider** traces circles. Mark layout lines with a **mechanical pencil**.

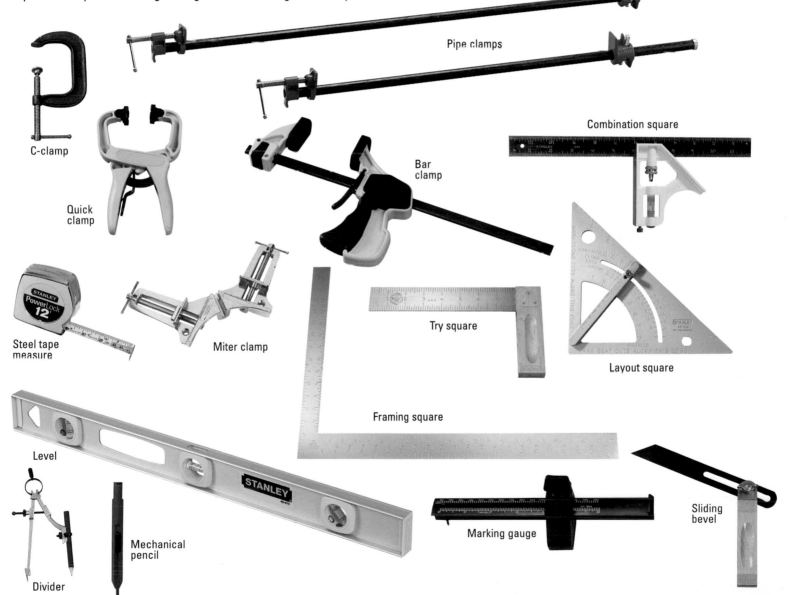

Pipe clamps

C-clamp

Quick clamp

Bar clamp

Combination square

Steel tape measure

Miter clamp

Try square

Layout square

Framing square

Level

Mechanical pencil

Marking gauge

Sliding bevel

Divider

POWER TOOLS

Portable power tools do basically the same jobs as their hand-tool counterparts, but they do them faster and usually more accurately. For accuracy, power, and durability, buy a name-brand, high-quality model rather than a discount, hobbyist one.

Sawing made quicker
One of the handiest tools you can own is a portable **circular saw,** which cuts lumber as well as plywood, with and across the grain. The gear-driven blades come in diameter sizes from 4 to 10 inches. The 7¼-inch size offers many blade options and is the most useful for do-it-yourself work. The better saws have ball bearings rather than sleeve bearings, and an arbor lock that holds the blade while you loosen it.

A **jigsaw** (also called a saber saw) cuts circles and curves as well as straight lines. Numerous blade types allow you to cut materials other than wood, such as metal and plastic. Variable speed control adds versatility; an orbiting feature helps with complicated scrolling but is less steady when making straight cuts.

Sanding made simpler
The **belt sander's** abrasive belt moves across a flat bed to remove wood quickly. Choose a sander with at least a 21-inch belt and a width you feel comfortable with—the wider the belt, the heavier the sander.

Orbital finishing sanders use an oscillating motion to move a portion of a sheet of sandpaper in tiny circles over the wood. The ¼-sheet size, called a **palm sander,** is popular. A **detail sander** allows you to smooth hard-to-reach areas, such as inside corners. A **random-orbit sander** uses a round abrasive disk that moves in a random pattern to remove stock faster than hand sanding, while reducing scratch marks. Models take 5- to 12-inch-diameter disks

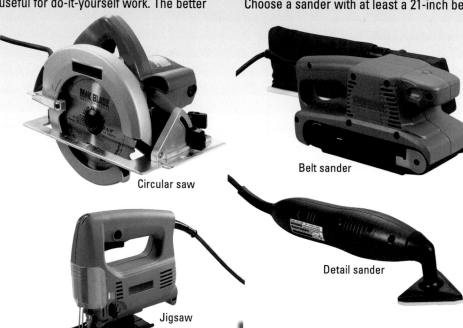

Circular saw

Belt sander

Jigsaw

Detail sander

Palm sander

Random-orbit sander

Look to the kitchen to clean blades

Common oven cleaner is an effective, safe, and inexpensive solvent for removing accumulated pitch and gum from saw blades. It's also less volatile than other gum removers.

Keep these three blades handy

Portable circular saws usually come equipped with a general-purpose blade that works well for most crosscutting and limited ripping. Add a 150-tooth hollow-ground plywood blade for smooth cuts in plywood panels, and a 24- to 30-tooth rip blade for making efficient cuts with the grain, and you'll be well-equipped.

Rip blade

Plywood blade

General purpose blade

that attach with adhesive or hook-and-loop fasteners. A good choice is a 5- or 6-inch-diameter model with dust collection.

Shaping is a snap

A **router** uses various spinning bits to shape board edges, cut grooves and slots (called dadoes and rabbets), create profile moldings, and much more. Available in horsepower ratings from less than one to three, routers have either a fixed base or are the "plunge" type (the housing slides up and down for starting and stopping cuts in the middle of a board). Bits come in ¼- or ½-inch-diameter shanks, the thicker being sturdier. Variable speed control isn't essential, but it can come in handy.

Drilling made faster

For drilling holes in wood and other materials, there's nothing handier than a **portable electric drill.** You'll find many types and styles, ranging from small cordless drill/screwdrivers to heavy-duty borers with a jack-hammer action for tackling concrete. Most models can turn in reverse for withdrawing screws, and many have torque control clutches that prevent the stripping of screw heads. Cordless models use rechargeable battery packs (up to about 18 volts), which add to their convenience, versatility, and their weight.

Electric drills are sold in ¼-, ⅜-, and ½-inch chuck sizes. A ⅜-inch variable speed reversing (VSR) cordless model with torque control is a workhorse tool for the home woodworker, combining high power with moderate price and weight.

Cleaning capably

The **shop vacuum** is indispensable for maintaining a tidy shop or work space. The largest hold about 28 gallons of debris; the smallest, under 5 gallons. Most vacs handle both dry and wet material; the better ones attach to woodworking power tools to collect dust at the source. Look for a model with high suction, a large-diameter hose that resists clogging, and a low whine—noise level doesn't indicate power.

Portable drill

Router

Shop vacuum

SAFETY FIRST
Don't let fashion dictate what you wear

Let safety be your guide when choosing what to wear when you work with hand and power tools. Wearing the wrong type of clothing can lead to accidents.

Protect your eyes with wraparound **safety glasses** or goggles. Full-face shields give optimum protection. When sanding, wear a **dust mask** that fits tightly around the nose and mouth. When using power tools, wear **hearing protection** such as ear plugs or muffs.

Wear a short-sleeved shirt, or roll up long sleeves so they won't get caught in moving parts. Remove all jewelry, too, especially bracelets, large rings, and watches. Never wear ties or neckerchiefs.To prevent slipping, wear rubber-soled shoes.

Keep a **push stick** handy when using a table saw. Always unplug a tool prior to cleaning it, changing blades, making adjustments, or leaving it unattended.

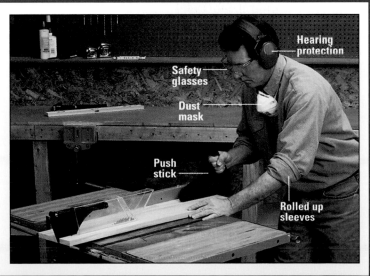

Hearing protection

Safety glasses

Dust mask

Push stick

Rolled up sleeves

STATIONARY POWER TOOLS

Serious amateur woodworkers move up to stationary power tools as they take on more and larger projects. These tools allow you to work faster and more accurately, but they also cost more money and take up more room. A good compromise is high-quality, bench-top power tools. They perform nearly as well as full-size stationary models but take up less space when in use and can be stored out of the way when not in use.

A **10-inch table saw** (blade size) cuts more accurately and has more accessories than a portable circular saw. A contractor-style table saw (with open legs) is usually the first large power tool a woodworker purchases—and the one likely to be used most often. A **compound miter saw** cuts angled pieces and makes crosscuts with precision. Those that accept 10-inch blades offer the greatest variety in blade types.

A **band saw** uses a thin band of blade to make intricate cuts, such as circles and scrolls. With a fence, it will also make straight cuts. Compared to a jigsaw, it's a precision tool.

A **router table** provides a router with stability and versatility. **Drill presses** improve boring accuracy, and those with attachments also can sand. A **planer** smooths the wide surfaces of rough-cut boards. A **jointer** straightens and smooths the edges of cut boards (especially useful when joining pieces) and will surface narrow boards.

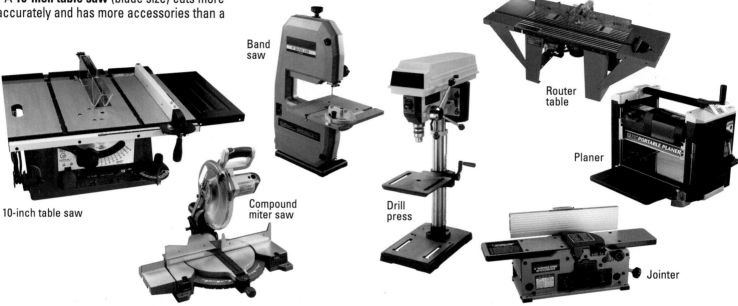

Band saw

Router table

Planer

10-inch table saw

Compound miter saw

Drill press

Jointer

CLEAN CUTS
Choose the right blade for the job

The most important part of a table saw is its blade. Carbide-tipped blades are the norm and fall into four basic tooth configurations: flat top (FT), alternate-top bevel (ATB), alternate-top bevel and raker (ATB&R), and triple chip (TC). Carbide blades in these configurations normally make a cut, called a kerf, about ⅛-inch wide. For minimizing waste when sawing expensive woods, buy thin-kerf blades, which make a cut about half as wide. Their thinner teeth won't allow as many sharpenings as a regular blade, though, so don't use them for general sawing.

Flat-top blades with 24 teeth provide fast, heavy-duty ripping capability. Alternate-top bevel blades with 40 teeth give plywood a smooth cut. ATB&R blades (called combination

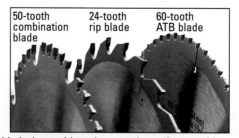

50-tooth combination blade   24-tooth rip blade   60-tooth ATB blade

blades) cut with and across the grain smoothly. Triple-chip blades tackle materials such as plastic laminate. With all blades, the more teeth, the smoother the cut.

The following three blades will cover most home woodworking tasks: a 50-tooth ATB&R or 40-tooth ATB; a 24-tooth FT rip blade, and 60- to 80-tooth ATB blade.

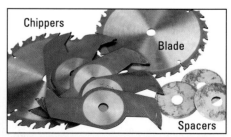

Chippers   Blade   Spacers

Dado blades and sets allow you to make a kerf up to about 1 inch wide in one pass. The sets include blades, which make the outside of the cut, and chippers, which remove material between the blades. Dado sets are expensive but leave a smoother kerf than a single adjustable dado blade, which "wobbles" at an angle to make a wide cut.

SET UP SHOP
Make the most of your work space

No matter what the size and shape of the space you have to work in, there are some planning points that you can follow to create a successful layout.

■ Divide the space into several machining areas. Identify all the steps you go through to make a project, then establish work stations near each power tool associated with them.

■ Plan for flexibility and mobility. Center a table saw at an angle in the shop to provide space for ripping long stock and sheet goods. Place it and other large tools on mobile bases so they can be easily moved as necessary.

■ Allow for moving materials and projects in and out. Don't block doorways with hard-to-move tools.

■ Leave work space between equipment. You'll need at least 30 inches between benches and stationary tools, and 20 inches for walkways.

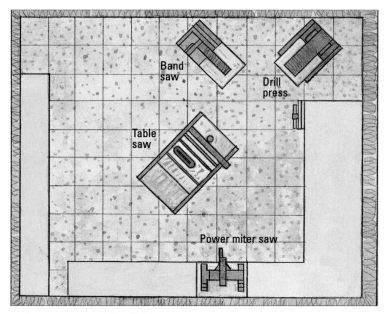

Typical basement plan: With mobile bases under the band saw, drill press, and table saw, you can move them into play as needed.

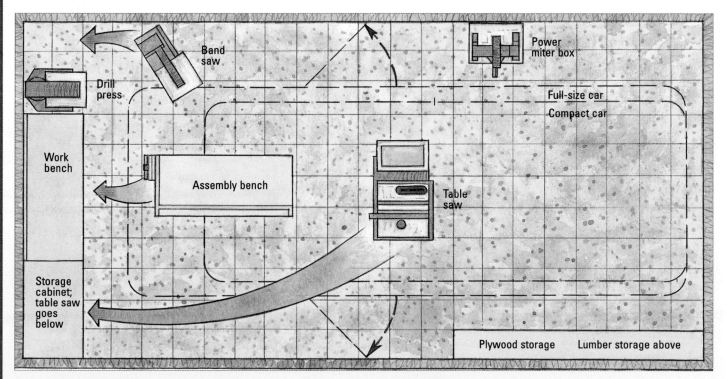

The garage shop: In either a single-car garage or half of a double one, you want to be able to roll out the machines when you need them and store them against the wall to make room for a car when they're not in use. Mobile bases make it possible.

ACCESSORIES

Power tools alone can do only so much—the accessories for them really expand their capabilities and simplify specific tasks. That's especially true for portable power tools—deck them out with well-chosen accessories and they'll do many of the same tasks expected of stationary ones. While you can buy many accessories at home centers, woodworking supply stores, or through mail-order, you can also make many of them yourself. Home-built accessories that hold or guide a tool to perform specific jobs quickly or accurately are called "jigs." See the example at the bottom of *page 19*.

One of the handiest accessories you can build is a reliable straightedge. With the one shown at right, you'll be able to accurately rip large sheets of plywood with a portable circular saw. Make another straightedge to serve as a guide for cutting dadoes, grooves, and rabbets with your router. With straightedges like these, you can quickly saw or rout precise cuts.

Building a straightedge

1 Glue and clamp a 2-inch-wide piece of ½-inch-thick stock to one edge of an equally long piece of ¼-inch plywood that's about 6 inches wider than your saw or router base. Both pieces should be a few inches longer than the longest cut you will make for your projects.

2 When the glue has dried, run the circular saw or the router with a straight-cutting bit along the ½-inch fence to rip the ¼-inch plywood to width. Using this jig guarantees a straight, accurate cut as long as you use the same blade or bit. Write the name of the tool and blade or bit on the jig.

Avoid underlit work, overloaded cords, and wobbly stock

It's difficult—and dangerous—to work in poorly lit areas. Portable, adjustable halogen work lights make sure you can see what you're doing.

To make sure your tools perform at peak power and to avoid dangerously overloaded extension cords, which can cause fires, use at least a 16-gauge extension cord with power tools that draw less than 10 amps, and a 14-gauge cord with ones that draw more.

A pair of sawhorses become workhorses when working with plywood. You can buy the brackets and make them yourself. A roller stand supports long pieces of material.

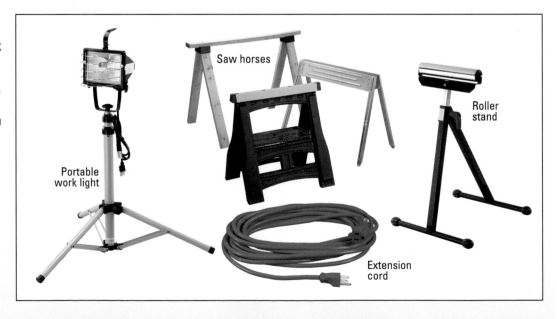

Saw horses

Roller stand

Portable work light

Extension cord

Good
portion

Waste
portion

3 To use the straightedge for crosscutting or ripping stock, draw your cut line with a fine lead pencil. Place the straightedge on top of the good portion of the material and carefully align its away-from-the-fence edge with the cut line. Secure the straightedge with clamps tightened on top of the fence and the bottom of the piece to be cut (and not impeding the tool's path). Run the saw or router against the fence to make the cut.

Crosscutting plywood

To crosscut plywood, support the sheet underneath with a network of 2×4s to hold up the stock on both sides of the cut. Draw your cut line and align the side opposite the fence with it, with the jig over the good portion of the stock. Use clamps on top of the fence at both ends of the straightedge to hold it tightly in place on the plywood. After double-checking alignment and support placement, make the cut.

STANLEY PRO TIP

Build a crosscutting jig for your portable circular saw

This jig makes clean, accurate crosscuts possible. Build the base by screwing and gluing a pair of parallel 1×2s to the top of a piece of 12-inch × 4-foot ¾-inch particleboard. Attach aluminum angle bars at 90 degrees to the 1×2s. Space them to fit the width of the circular saw's base plate. Adjust the saw blade so it cuts through the 1×2s and makes a slight kerf (cut) in the base.

To use the jig, clamp it to your workbench, slip the board to be cut under the guide bars, hold or clamp it in place, and make the cut. Rub paraffin on the aluminum angle bars to help the saw slide more easily.

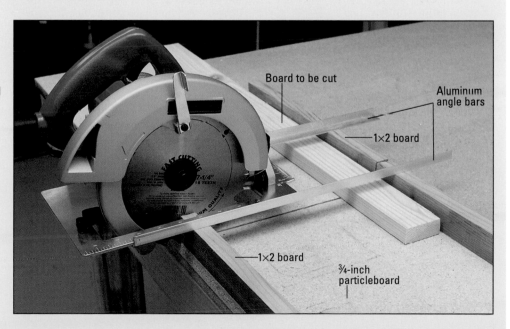

Board to be cut

Aluminum
angle bars

1×2 board

1×2 board

¾-inch
particleboard

MATERIALS & HARDWARE

You put a lot of craftsmanship and time into your projects, so you want to use the right materials for the job. As with buying tools, always try to purchase the highest quality material and hardware your budget allows, as appropriate for your project's intended use. For instance, you'd waste money buying a fine hardwood, such as cherry, for a utilitarian bookcase that's going to sit in a basement or workshop.

Know your stock
This chapter helps you decide what materials to choose for what purposes. You'll learn the differences between hardwoods and softwoods, when and where to use each type, and how to select them. You'll find out about the special properties of plywood, the many grades and types it comes in, and how to shop for it wisely. We'll also discuss and compare other composite sheet goods, such as oriented strand board, particleboard, and fiberboard. And we'll share tips from the pros on how best to make use of each type of material.

Understand the hardware
Walking the hardware aisles at a large home center can be overwhelming. This chapter will guide you through various types of fasteners.

And fasteners are just one category of hardware. No less puzzling is the variety of hinges, shelf brackets, and other products that help you assemble wood into functional pieces of case furniture and shelving. We'll familiarize you with these as well.

Finish off the project
Finally you'll discover the materials experts use to give the finishing touches to bookcases and shelves—the magic, easy-to-use product that makes an inexpensive piece of plywood look like a costly solid board, for example. Or how to employ moldings to give simple boxes a degree of finish and flair that makes them a source of craftsmanlike pride as well as practical functionality. Many cabinet- and furniture-making solutions are quite simple. We'll equip you with the material know-how you need to get the kinds of results you'll be proud to showcase in your home.

Materials for furniture-quality projects differ from those for carpentry.

CHAPTER PREVIEW

Lumber
page 22

Plywood
page 24

Composites
page 26

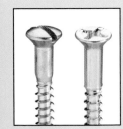
Fasteners
page 28

Hardware
page 30

Edge banding
page 32

Molding
page 33

Selecting the wood and hardware from all that's available is a fun part of woodworking that most people look forward to. But buying the materials it takes to make your project the best it can be takes some savvy. A little bit of knowledge goes far in giving you a greater appreciation and enjoyment of the craft.

LUMBER

The lumber used to make furniture-quality projects differs from the dimensional lumber used in building construction in several ways. It's drier (less than 9 percent moisture content), has fewer defects (the number depends on the grade), and costs more. The first step to becoming a savvy lumber shopper is to learn the difference between softwoods and hardwoods.

Softwood

Commonly available lumber made from softwood species, such as those shown at right, is cut from coniferous evergreen trees, which do not drop their needles each year.

Of the many types of softwoods, the following are most readily available:

■ **Western red cedar:** Attractive, aromatic, and naturally weather-resistant.
■ **White pine:** Clear boards can be naturally finished. Stains blotch.
■ **Redwood:** Attractive and naturally weather-resistant.
■ **Douglas fir:** Strong and hard.
■ **Spruce:** Inexpensive and paintable.
■ **Northern white cedar:** Light and naturally weather-resistant.

Softwoods are both lighter and softer than hardwoods, making them easier to work with. The best softwood lumber for furniture construction is listed in the chart at the bottom of *page 23*.

Redwood and western red cedar lumber are sold a bit differently from other softwoods. They're graded both by appearance and by the amount of decay-resistant heartwood the boards contain—the more, the better. *Clear all-heart* is the most costly; *construction common* the least.

Softwood boards of 1-inch thickness—the type you'd use for bookcases and shelves—are sold in 2-inch-width increments, such as 1×2, 1×4, etc. You pay for it by the running foot. Home centers usually group softwood boards in bins labeled by width and length. The sizes shown are "nominal," as explained in the Pro Tip on *page 23*.

You won't want to use boards that display any of the major defects illustrated below, especially those that are warped. To check a board for warp, lay it on the floor and see if it lies flat. Also check for knots, but worry only about loose ones—they'll have a visible dark line around them and will work loose and eventually drop out. Tight knots, on the other hand, are structurally sound but must be coated with a sealer before painting so they don't weep sap and discolor the paint.

Redwood

White pine

Northern white cedar

Douglas fir

Spruce

Western red cedar

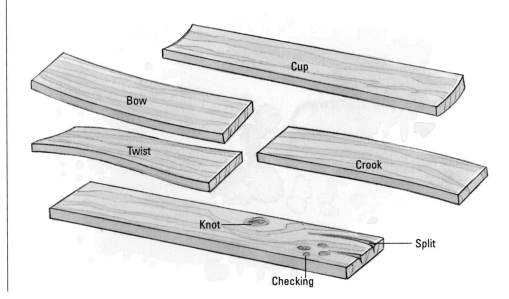

Bow

Cup

Twist

Crook

Knot

Split

Checking

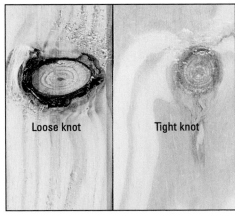

Loose knot

Tight knot

Avoid boards with loose knots such as the one above left. Loose knots often fall out as the wood dries, leaving a hole. Tight knots such as the one above right are acceptable but need sealing.

Hardwood

Produced by broad-leafed, deciduous trees that—in the world's temperate zone—lose their leaves each year, hardwoods get the nod for cabinets and furniture because of their beauty, stability, strength, machining predictability, and resistance to abuse. Here are some woodworking favorites:

■ **Red oak:** A classic for furniture and cabinets, it is easy to work.
■ **White ash:** Strong and hard.
■ **Walnut:** Deep color, nice grain.
■ **Yellow poplar:** Fairly strong but plain. Best for painting; will stain to mimic cherry or walnut.
■ **Cherry:** Hard, strong, and beautiful.
■ **Philippine mahogany:** Imported and hard to find but easy to work and stain to imitate real mahogany.

In North America, hardwood trees are not as abundant as softwood trees, making their lumber more valuable. That's also why hardwood logs are sawed to minimize waste, resulting in boards of varying quality. Because of that, hardwood boards are assigned grades, as noted in the chart below. The higher, costlier grades yield more defect-free (clear) material.

There's also a major difference in the way hardwoods are sold. You buy them by the board foot. That's a volume measurement of thickness, width, and length that equals 144 cubic inches. A board measuring 1×12×12 inches equals one board foot. You seldom have to do those calculations, though; most retail hardwood outlets, including home centers, have already done so before pricing their boards. Typically, board footage is rounded up or down to the nearest one-half board foot.

Woodworkers usually refer to hardwood board thickness in ¼-inch increments. A 1-inch-thick board is called $\frac{4}{4}$; a 1¼-inch-thick one, $\frac{5}{4}$; a 2-inch one, $\frac{8}{4}$, and so on.

Hardwoods (and the best softwood grades) are also kiln-dried at a controlled temperature to reduce their moisture content to 6–9 percent, the ideal range for interior projects. Kiln-dried lumber won't readily reabsorb moisture when coated properly with a finish. That means it will remain stable in use and will be less likely to swell, shrink, crack, or warp over time.

Walnut

Philippine mahogany

Cherry

White ash

Yellow poplar

Red oak

LUMBER GRADES

Here's what the grades of hardwood and softwood lumber mean:

HARDWOODS

First and seconds (FAS)	Best grade. Boards yield 83⅓% clear wood
Selects	One side FAS, other No 1. common. Same yield as FAS on one side
No. 1 common	Economical. Boards yield 66⅔% clear cuttings one side

SOFTWOODS

C select & better	Minor imperfections
D select	A few sound defects
3rd clear	Well-placed knots allow for clear cuttings
No. 1 shop	More knots and fewer clear cuts than 3rd clear
No. 2, No. 3 common	Utility shelving grades. No. 2 has fewer and smaller knots

STANLEY PRO TIP

Know what you're paying for

With hardwoods, you pay for a board's full thickness, but you actually get less because of planing. A rough board that's 1 inch thick measures $\frac{13}{16}$ inch after surfacing two sides (S2S).

Softwoods follow this measuring system as well. Keep in mind that due to milling, a "nominal" size 1×2 board becomes ¾×1½ inch actual size; a 1×4 is ¾×3½ inches; a 1×6 equals ¾×5½ inches; and a 2×4 ends up being 1½×3½ inches.

PLYWOOD

Gluing thin pieces of wood together to form a thicker one was used by ancient Egyptians, but plywood as we know it was born in the 20th century.

A 4×8-foot sheet of plywood is typically made up of an uneven number of thin wood layers, or plies, glued together with their grain running at right angles to one another. This cross-banded construction gives plywood great strength in all directions. It also results in extra dimensional stability—plywood doesn't swell or crack like solid sawed lumber. Plywood also has another big advantage: It's available in panels wider than natural boards and in thicknesses ranging from ⅛ to 1¼ inches in ⅛-inch increments.

Two types of **softwood plywood** are manufactured: interior, which is assembled with moisture-resistant glue, and exterior, which is made with 100 percent waterproof glue. All softwood plywood is sold in appearance grades with letter designations, with "A" being the highest quality. The two sides may carry different grades, such as "A-C."

Hardwood plywood differs from the softwood variety in that its face and back veneers are of a hardwood species such as red oak or maple. It is also assembled to best display grain (see chart, *page 25)* and is strictly for interior use.

Softwood plywood

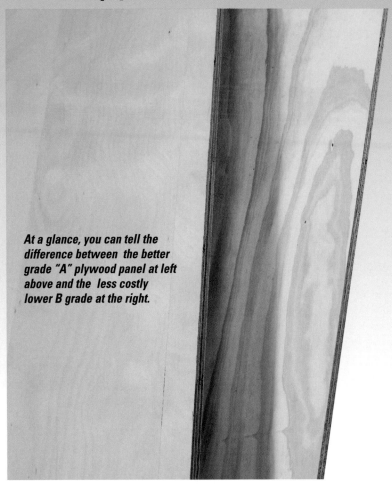

At a glance, you can tell the difference between the better grade "A" plywood panel at left above and the less costly lower B grade at the right.

STANLEY PRO TIP

Get plywood edges smooth and paintable

Softwood plywood usually gets a coat of paint, but glued-up plies showing on the edges pose a problem because they're rough and often have gaps. You can apply wood putty as filler, but it requires heavy sanding. Exterior spackling compound is cheaper, dries more quickly, sands easier, and works just as well.

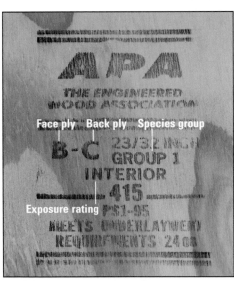

Grade stamps on plywood tell you the quality of face and back plies (letters A through D) and its exposure rating.

The defects on softwood plywood include football-shaped plugs where knots were removed and filled, and gaps between plies.

Hardwood plywood

Hardwood plywood graded A-Premium is the most costly and attractive. The top sheet (left) is oak veneer; the bottom (right) is birch veneer.

THE BEST HARDWOOD PLYWOOD GRADES

Grades differ by veneer quality and number and size of defects allowed.

Grade	Qualities
A-Premium	Sliced veneers matched for pleasing color and grain, one-piece rotary cut. Pin knots, small patches not allowed
1-Good (cabinet grade)	Unmatched veneers OK. No sharp contrasts in color, grain, or figure. Burls, pin knots, and small patches allowed
2-Sound	No figure, color, or grain match. Smooth patches, sound knots, and discoloration or varying color allowed

Other designations may be dealer-applied.

JUDGING HARDWOOD PLYWOOD
Show the best side

Premium grades of hardwood plywood—AA, A, and A1—pose a problem when selecting which side to show on a project. Both sides may appear identical, but there are subtle differences.

The best side has even color, consistent grain, no flaws, and the fewest visible splices. In the photos at right, the top panel has fewer splices and a better grain pattern than the other premium-grade panel.

COMPOSITES

Plywood isn't the only workable material available in sheets. Today's forest products industry seeks to minimize waste by using every ounce of wood—from wood chips and flakes to sawdust—in the manufacture of sheet goods that are generally called "composite wood products."

Oriented strand board (OSB) has bonded wood chips laid up in layers, each running in a different direction. Although nearly as strong as plywood, its rough surface texture generally limits its use to utility shelving.

Particleboard employs glued sawdust and tiny chips. It's hard and fairly smooth but easily sags under load, can fracture, and swells when wet.

Melamine-covered particleboard has a plasticlike coating that eliminates finishing. Otherwise it has the same characteristics as uncoated particleboard.

Medium-density fiberboard (MDF) uses very fine wood fibers for an extremely smooth surface. It's stronger than particleboard and moisture-resistant. However, it sometimes splits when nailed.

Medium-density
fiberboard (MDF)

Melamine-covered
particleboard

Particleboard

Oriented strand
board (OSB)

STANLEY PRO TIP: **Stand sheet goods to save space**

Sheet goods take up less space when stored on end. They're also handier to move in this position.

To slide them out easily, build an edged platform from plastic-laminate-covered stock (a piece of countertop works nicely). Hang a tilt-stop, made of 2×4 material, from the exposed overhead joists. This will catch the outside sheets when you pull out an inner one.

An easily constructed rack like this one makes storing and pulling sheet goods a simple matter.

SAGLESS SPANS

Sagless spans are the goal for traditional, living-room-style shelving. Each type of material has a different span limit, i.e., the maximum distance it can span between supports without sagging or breaking under a load.

According to architect calculations, books represent an average load of 25 pounds per cubic foot. At right, you can see the no-sag span limit under load of the most commonly used shelving materials.

Solid hardwood has the best no-sag rating; however, some species are stiffer than others. Birch, maple, and oak are the stiffest, followed by ash, cherry, and walnut.

You can increase the stiffness of a shelf by sinking screws into it through the solid back of the case. Or, as shown below, add more strength and maintain adjustability by attaching a cleat or molding to the front of the shelf. Aprons can also be added under the shelf.

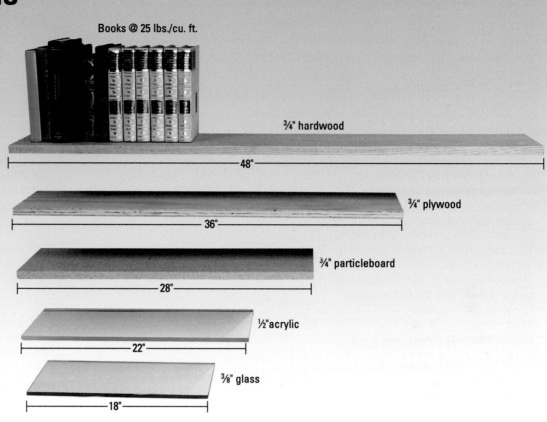

Books @ 25 lbs./cu. ft.

¾" hardwood — 48"

¾" plywood — 36"

¾" particleboard — 28"

½" acrylic — 22"

⅜" glass — 18"

STURDY SHELVES
Four ways to increase spans

Aprons or additional pieces: Increase a wooden shelf's span limit by fastening wood-matched 1×2 aprons underneath (top) or simply by using two plywood pieces (bottom).

Railing: Cut a rabbet into a piece of solid molding and attach it as a "railing" that conceals the plywood edge and adds support.

Molding: Simply attach a 1×2 molding to the shelf's front edge. This method also hides the unsightly edge.

FASTENERS

In order to assemble woodworking projects, you need to acquaint yourself with a variety of fasteners. These include wood screws, brads, nails, and adhesives.

Screws

Common wood screws are made of steel and normally have a rust-resistant zinc coating. Flat-head wood screws (FHWS) are made to be driven flush with the surface. You also can counterbore them into a hole in the surface and cover the screw with either a wood plug or wood putty so the fastener is hidden. Oval-head and round-head wood screws (RHWS) protrude above the surface for decorative effect or a finished look when

fastening metal hardware. You'll also choose from three common screw-head slot types: slotted, phillips, and square drive. These match different screwdriving tools.

Lag screws are heavy-duty fasteners that have a threaded shank like a wood screw and a hex-head like a machine bolt that allows you to use a wrench, rather than a screwdriver, to apply more torque when tightening them. Hanger screws have a wood-screw thread on one end and a machine-screw thread on the other, allowing you to screw one end into a wall stud, for example, and use a nut and bolt on the other. Both of these specialty fasteners are useful when attaching heavy cabinets to a wall.

Case-hardened steel screws, often called drywall screws, have a skinny shank and a dull black finish. They're exceptionally tough and are most often used with a power drill-driver. Case-hardened screws come in two thread configurations. One-thread single-leads hold best in softwoods and particleboard. Double-leads have twin threads that bite into hardwoods better. A trim-head screw is a thin, case-hardened double-lead screw with a small head that acts like a finishing nail when fastening trim.

Screw sizes are a breeze to understand. Their gauge denotes the size of their shank diameter in a range from #0 (smallest) to #24 (largest). Gauge increases about 1/64 inch

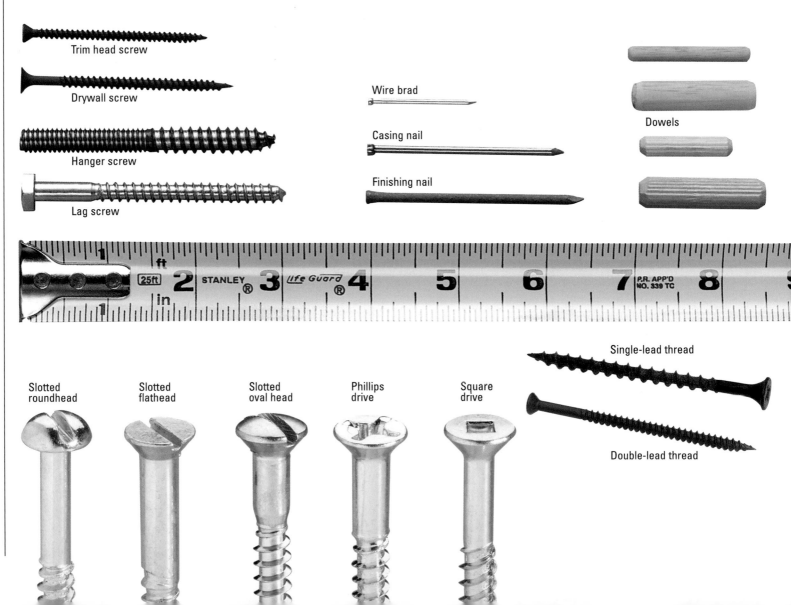

Trim head screw

Drywall screw

Hanger screw

Lag screw

Wire brad

Casing nail

Finishing nail

Dowels

Slotted roundhead

Slotted flathead

Slotted oval head

Phillips drive

Square drive

Single-lead thread

Double-lead thread

in each size increment. Lengths begin at ¼ inch and extend to 4 inches and longer. Each length comes in three or more gauges. The thinner the wood, the smaller gauge screw you need.

Other fasteners

Some joinery uses wooden **dowels,** coated with glue and inserted into holes, to join components together. You can buy them in various diameters and lengths.

Finishing nails are thin, small-headed nails used for fastening molding and other interior trim. The heads are usually countersunk below the wood surface. The resulting hole

is then filled with wood filler. Use **casing nails** where the heads will be exposed to moisture. **Brads** have heads like finishing nails but are much smaller.

Used to reinforce joints, **mending plates** and **brackets** are screwed in places where they won't be seen.

Glues

Although many types of adhesives are on the market, including epoxies and "super glues," the best all-purpose glue for most woodworking is aliphatic resin (AR) glue, and modified formulas of it. Those glues are premixed, so you apply them from squeeze-

bottle containers. They come in white (PVA), yellow, and darker tints for dark woods. They're strong, and they dry in about three hours. (The white variety dries more slowly, giving you extended time to work.) Newer formulas provide extended water resistance. Shelf life is about six months to a year if refrigerated (but not frozen) when not in use.

Polyurethane glue is gaining favor with some woodworkers because it performs much like epoxy without the mixing and the strong chemical odor. It's waterproof too. You'll pay more, however, for polyurethane than AR glue.

SHOP REFERENCE GUIDE FOR SCREWS

Typical uses	Attaching small hardware					General assembly			Heavy-duty assembly		
Gauge	2	3	4	5	6	7	8	9	10	12	14
Head bore size	¹¹⁄₆₄"	¹³⁄₆₄"	¹⁵⁄₆₄"	¼"	⁹⁄₃₂"	⁵⁄₁₆"	¹¹⁄₃₂"	²³⁄₆₄"	²⁵⁄₆₄"	⁷⁄₁₆"	½"
Shank drill size	³⁄₃₂"	⁷⁄₆₄"	⁷⁄₆₄"	⅛"	⁹⁄₆₄"	⁵⁄₃₂"	⁵⁄₃₂"	¹¹⁄₆₄"	³⁄₁₆"	⁷⁄₃₂"	¼"
Pilot drill size	¹⁄₁₆"	¹⁄₁₆"	⁵⁄₆₄"	⁵⁄₆₄"	³⁄₃₂"	⁷⁄₆₄"	⁷⁄₆₄"	⅛"	⅛"	⁹⁄₆₄"	⁵⁄₃₂"

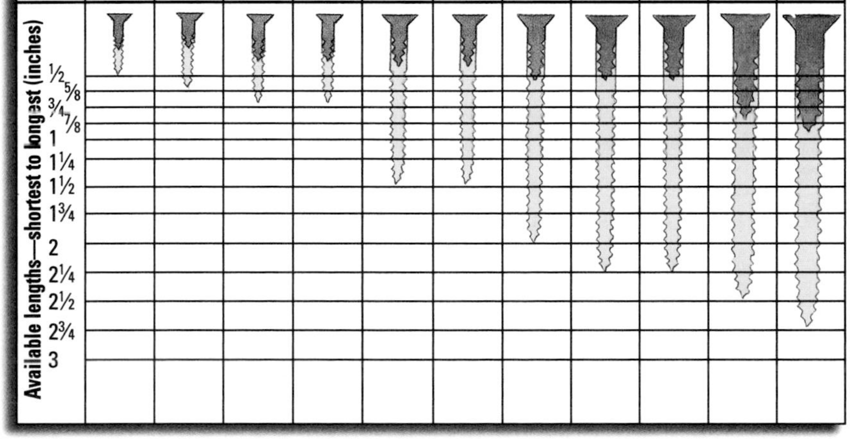

Available lengths—shortest to longest (inches): ½, ⅝, ¾, ⅞, 1, 1¼, 1½, 1¾, 2, 2¼, 2½, 2¾, 3

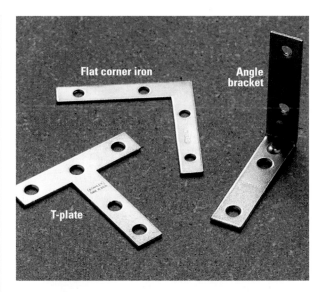

Flat corner iron   Angle bracket   T-plate

The best all-purpose wood glue is aliphatic resin (AR) glue. Spread glue on parts with a stiff bristle or foam brush.

HARDWARE

When you opt to build adjustable shelves, the hardware you choose depends upon the type of shelving you're going to build.

Open shelving
Often called "utility" shelving because it plays an important storage role in a basement, garage, or laundry room, open shelving—shelves attached directly to a wall rather than built into a case—can be dressed up for the den and living room too. Getting the look you want begins with **shelf standards**. These metal tracks are made in various styles and finishes. They're either fastened directly to the wall or mounted in wall-attached wood channels. To carry heavy loads, mount them to the wall studs with heavy screws or lag bolts. For lighter loads, you can use hollow-wall anchors or toggle bolts.

Some styles of standards only accept **metal shelf brackets.** Others are designed for decorative, wooden **corbel-type brackets.** Another type, usually used in cabinets, takes only **metal clips.** Dress your shelves up or down by selecting the appropriate design and finish.

Encased shelving
When building adjustable shelves inside a bookcase or cabinet, you can support the shelves where they meet the sides of the piece in one of three ways: using surface-mounted standards, standards flush-mounted in a groove, or **pin supports**.

Wood dowels can be used as pin supports, and there are dozens of metal and plastic varieties available as well. All pin supports require two rows of evenly spaced ¼-inch or 5 mm holes on each side of the cabinet or case.

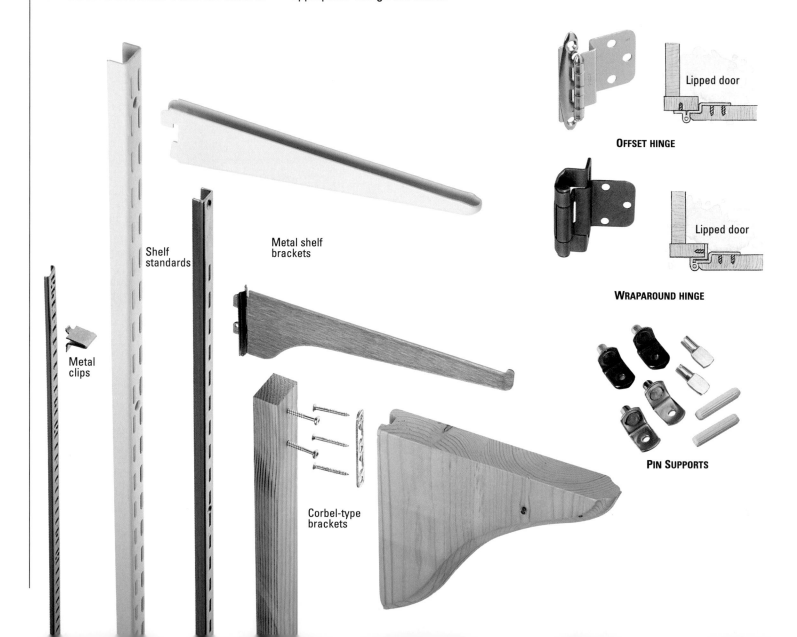

Metal clips

Shelf standards

Metal shelf brackets

Corbel-type brackets

OFFSET HINGE

Lipped door

Lipped door

WRAPAROUND HINGE

PIN SUPPORTS

If you plan to add doors and drawers to a bookcase, you'll have to get to know other types of hardware as well. Door catches, hinges, pulls, and drawer slides are so numerous in configuration, finish, and style that all the varieties fill catalogs. Start by learning the basic types.

Lipped doors—doors that partially cover the cabinet's frame—generally require one of two hinge types. The **offset hinge** fastens to the face frame and the back of the door. A **wraparound hinge** is attached to the back of the door and the inside edge of the face frame. They're used on overlapped doors, too. For doors without lips that either cover, partially cover, or fit flush with the cabinet face, you have several options.

A **cylinder-style hinge** mounts to the face frame and into a recess cut in the back of a door. **Pivot hinges,** attached to the back of an overlapped door and the face frame, are concealed. A **semiconcealed hinge** attaches the same way but to a partially overlapped door. For a flush door, use a **butt hinge** that folds between the door and face frame. Growing in popularity is the **Eurostyle hinge,** which fastens to the door back and cabinet side.

To open doors and to keep them closed, handles and catches are used. Handles come in many forms, colors, and finishes but fall into only two categories: **pulls** and **knobs.** Both require drilling through the door, then attaching the hardware with screws. Catches tightly hold doors closed and are available in several common styles including **friction** and **magnetic** catches.

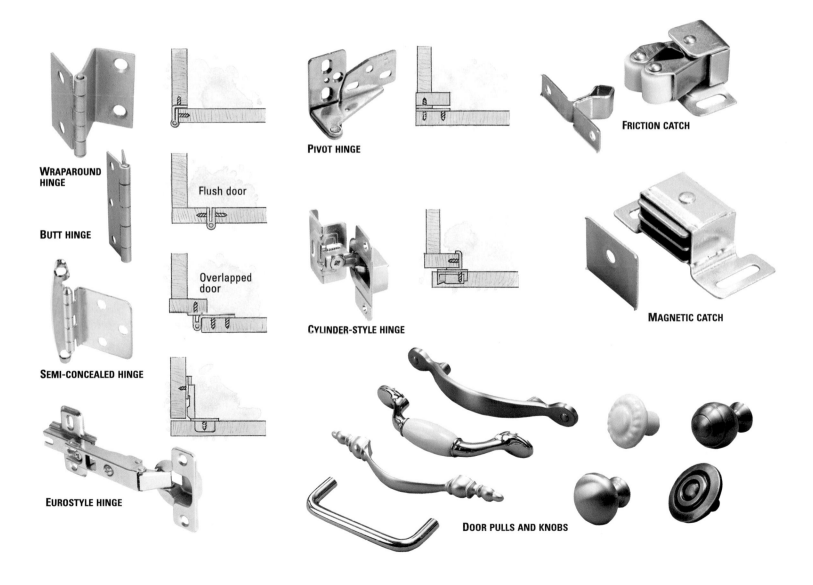

WRAPAROUND HINGE

BUTT HINGE

SEMI-CONCEALED HINGE

EUROSTYLE HINGE

Flush door

Overlapped door

PIVOT HINGE

CYLINDER-STYLE HINGE

FRICTION CATCH

MAGNETIC CATCH

DOOR PULLS AND KNOBS

EDGE BANDING

Before applying a finish to a bookcase or shelf project made from plywood or other sheet goods, you must decide what to do with the exposed edges. They're normally rough, and with plywood, the visible plies detract from the project's aesthetic appeal.

For a plywood project that you plan to paint, fill and sand the exposed edge *(page 56)*. When working with melamine-coated MDF, use preglued melamine edge banding. It's available in almond or white. Simply cut it to length and iron it in place.

A bookcase or shelf made from furniture-quality hardwood plywood calls for a different approach. One is to cut and attach molding *(page 33)* or thin, solid wood strips. A quicker course is the application of wood-veneer edge banding. Like the melamine variety, wood edge banding is preglued with hot-melt adhesive, making it easy to iron in place. Its 1/100-inch thickness makes it flexible, yet it won't crack because it's tenderized. You can buy the presanded, 3/4-inch-wide material in your favorite hardwoods: cherry, mahogany, maple, oak, and walnut.

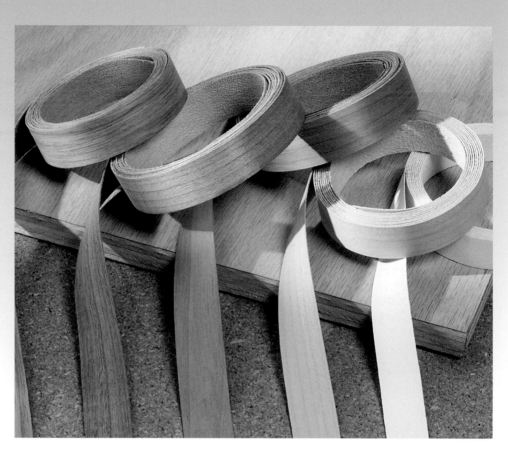

APPLYING EDGE BANDING
Two quick and easy steps to great-looking edges

You'll be amazed at how easy it is to finish the edges of hardwood plywood shelves and cases. All you need are a roll of wood veneer edge banding, a sharp utility knife, a ruler, and a household iron set on medium-low heat, no steam. (Use an old iron; you won't want to iron clothing with it after this.)

Measure the length of each edge that needs covering. Cut banding strips to rough length with the crafts knife. Position on the edge, check that the glued side is down (the grain is less distinct on the glued side), and press evenly and firmly with the iron (left).

If you have corners to cover, the job will look neater if you miter-cut them. Overlap the two pieces that will join. Hold them in place as you make a clean 45-degree cut through both pieces (right). Doing so ensures the ends will match perfectly when you iron the strips in place.

MOLDING

Molding not only conceals unsightly shelf edges, it adds a decorative touch. It's also a way to hide gaps and dress up built-ins and other projects when you don't have the power tools to create shaped wood yourself.

Although most molding profiles were created for specific purposes, they come in dozens of styles that can be adapted for a variety of uses. Note that although oak moldings are shown here, you'll find them in other hardwoods and in less costly paintable and stainable composite materials as well. Here are some available styles:

■ **Baseboard molding** covers the gap between the floor and a built-in such as a bookcase. Select a profile that matches the baseboard in your home.

■ **Strips** conceal plywood edges and also can be used to add strength to shelves. Strips are usually available in 1-inch thickness up to 4 inches wide.

■ **Crown molding** is used to finish the top of a built-in and covers the gap between it and the ceiling.

■ **Cove molding** is a plainer version of crown.

■ **Door-edge molding** is used to give hardwood plywood doors and drawers the appearance of solid wood panel construction.

■ **Base cap molding** provides an appealing edge for shelves.

■ **Base shoe molding** conceals gaps on all sides of a built-in. It's flexible, so it conforms to irregular floors and walls.

■ **Ornamental moldings** are embossed for a handcrafted look.

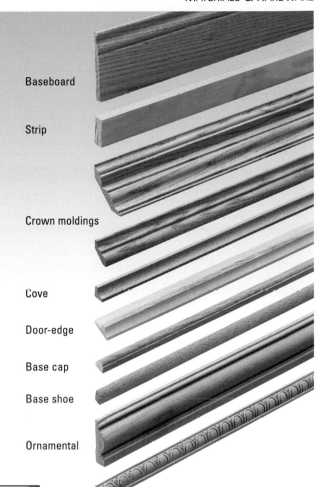

Baseboard

Strip

Crown moldings

Cove

Door-edge

Base cap

Base shoe

Ornamental

TRANSFORM WITH TRIM
Add moldings to increase visual appeal

If there's a problem associated with moldings, it's deciding which ones to use. Crisp, clean profiles contribute to plain, contemporary lines, while ornate ones relate to antique and traditional styles. The contrast can be dramatic, as shown in the two self-edge treatments, top. So select moldings that complement your home's decor.

A colonial profile casing in oak, middle, becomes the cornice on an entertainment center. The unit's doors, bottom, were trimmed with door-edge molding.

Add smaller moldings by gluing and clamping. Larger moldings are best fastened with finishing nails. Sink the heads of finishing nails below the surface and conceal them with putty.

STANLEY PRO TIP

No long clamps?

If your clamps fall short of spanning the width of a plywood shelf to hold a trim piece while the glue dries, look to masking tape. When the glue has dried and you remove the tape, wipe off the tape's adhesive residue with a little solvent, such as lacquer thinner.

MASTERING BASIC SKILLS

Maybe you've done some home repair or even a bit of remodeling. If so, you've already acquired many of the basic skills needed to build bookcases and shelves. What you'll learn in this chapter will add to that knowledge. If you're just getting started as a do-it-yourselfer, this is must-read information to build on as you accomplish your first project, then another.

In previous chapters, you learned about hand and power tools and what they do and about the materials and hardware available. In this chapter, you'll see how tools and materials come together to create beautiful, practical pieces of furniture that you and your family will enjoy for years to come. Read carefully, then practice the skills on scrap wood,

always with common sense and safety in mind.

Building skills
The first few pages tell you how to lay out, measure, and mark precisely. The old woodworking adage, "Measure twice, cut once," is a truism that many have discovered only after wasting material.

Following that introduction, you learn how to craft straight cuts with hand and power tools in both boards and sheet goods. If the words "rip" and "crosscut" are new to you, they soon won't be. (Ripping simply means cutting wood with the grain, crosscutting, as the word implies, means cutting wood at right angles to the grain.)

You'll also read up on how to cut precise angles and smooth curves. In the process, you'll get to know a sliding bevel, a tool for accurately duplicating angles when making cuts, and a miter box, an accessory that will help you make those cuts by hand with precision.

Drilling may seem boring (pun intended!), but there are several kinds of tools and accessories that will help you create clean, smooth holes more easily and accurately than ever before.

Using a chisel, one of the oldest tools around, is almost a lost art these days. We'll show you how to properly use one so it can help you make some strong, tight-fitting, handcrafted joinery that sets your project apart from—and probably outlast—much machine-made furniture found in stores.

It's not the tools that make the project— it's the skill with which they're used.

CHAPTER PREVIEW

Layout and marking
page 36

Straight cuts
page 38

Angled and curved cuts
page 40

Building adjustable shelves requires drilling lots of precisely spaced holes of exactly the same depth. Here's a trick that makes that task easy, fast, and accurate: Clamp a piece of pegboard squarely and securely to your work. Using the pegboard's holes as a guide, drill the holes in your stock. A drill stop controls each hole's depth.

Drilling
page 42

Chiseling
page 43

LAYOUT AND MARKING

Never take dimensions for granted when working with boards and sheet goods. That goes for squareness too.

Due to super-fast milling processes, shrinkage, and other factors, board ends may be out of square. Boards may also taper slightly along their length.

Normally you can count on a 4×8-foot sheet of plywood to have true edges, but check it for squareness and measure its thickness. A ¾-inch-thick sheet may be slightly off—a good reason to buy all the plywood you'll need from the same batch at the same time. If they're not all the precise dimensions they're supposed to be, chances are they'll at least be uniform in thickness.

To measure accurately every time, use the same tape measure throughout the building of a project. Furniture making requires precision; use a mechanical pencil, which makes a finer line. If you use a carpenter's pencil, mark with the narrow edge of the lead.

Check for square: Always check a board's end for squareness before measuring and marking other cuts. Put the handle of a try square against the edge of the board with its blade across the end. Any light between them indicates the board is out of square. Mark the board and cut it square.

Measure for length: Use a steel tape to measure and mark for cuts to length. Make one measurement on each board edge, then join them by marking along a try square.

Can you trust your tape?

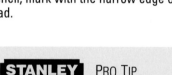

Tape measures become inaccurate if the rivet holes in the end get elongated. If that happens, line up the 1-inch mark with the squared end of the board, then subtract an inch from the tape reading when marking at the other end. Better yet, avoid confusion—replace the tape! And always use the same tape.

CUTTING THE LONG WAY
Use a marking gauge

Marking materials for ripping (cutting a board down its length with the grain, or plywood in its long dimension) requires great accuracy. If you have a straightedge that's long enough, use it. If you have a table saw, you don't need a guideline to follow. Simply set the fence away from the blade to the width of the cut, then feed the material through.

For cut lines in boards or narrow rips in plywood, many woodworkers turn to a marking gauge. Its thumbscrew-adjustable fence slides along one edge of the material while a sharp pin set in its post scribes the cut line. The post length determines maximum width.

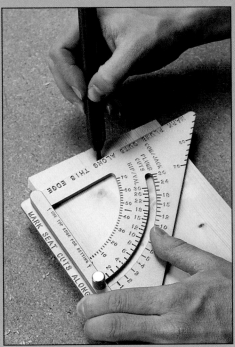

Mark with a V: Rather than making a simple straight-line pencil mark, make a V-shape mark with its point exactly on the tape measurement you want. You're less likely to lose track of a mark like this.

Use a layout square: A try square works fine for marking crosscuts, but its blade sometimes gets out of square. Whenever possible, use a layout square. Then your marks will always be perpendicular to the edge.

Marking large sheets: To mark a sheet of plywood for a cut across its width, you'll need a straightedge at least 4 feet long *(page 18)*. After measuring and marking each end of the cutoff line, clamp the straightedge in place at the marks. Then draw your line.

CUTTING DIAGRAMS
Make the most of materials

When you're faced with a project that has many parts, a cutting diagram will keep waste to a minimum. It also helps you maximize the use of grain for appearance because you'll be able to visualize how each part fits into the finished project.

Select which side of the material you wish to show (to choose the best side of plywood, see *page 39*). Then follow the Bill of Materials provided with your project plan and lay out parts directly on the wood. Draw light, erasable pencil lines. Assign a part number to each piece, write the numbers on masking tape labels, and attach them to the wood. That way, you can use a dark marker for greater visibility without having to erase pencil marks later. When marking cuts, make an allowance for the kerf—the material removed by the blade as it cuts—so your pieces aren't undersized.

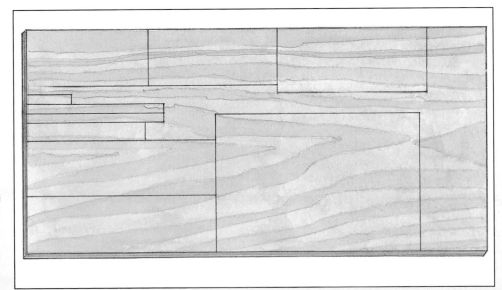

STRAIGHT CUTS

In woodworking, you'll spend lots of time reducing large pieces of wood to smaller ones. The straight cuts you make fall into two categories: rips and crosscuts.

A rip reduces the width of a piece of stock. In the case of a board, it's a cut along the length in the direction of the grain. In the case of plywood and other sheet goods, it's a cut along the sheet's long dimension, no matter the direction of the grain. Normally ripping stock to width is the first "machining" step in woodworking.

After stock has been ripped to the width desired, it's cut to length with a crosscut. This is done across (perpendicular to) the board's grain or in the narrow dimension of plywood and other sheet goods. Same-length parts should be sawed in one sequence (especially with power saws) with the assistance of a stop. A stop is a piece of wood clamped in place to limit travel of the stock being cut beyond the required length. Using a stop eliminates remeasuring *(page 86)*.

STANLEY PRO TIP

Saving the face of plywood's thin veneers

Hardwood plywood faced with veneers of cherry, oak, maple, and walnut is expensive, so always use a specially made plywood rip blade when cutting it with circular saws. These blades usually have about 55 alternately beveled teeth and therefore make the cleanest cuts.

Face veneers differ too. American-made hardwood veneers are from 1/28 inch to 1/32 inch thick. Asian veneers may only be 1/100. To reduce the possibility of chipping them, apply masking tape over the area to be sawed, then saw through the tape.

Ripping

A portable circular saw makes ripping boards fairly easy. Support the board with 2×4s underneath and clamp a guide in place. A kerf splitter behind the saw keeps the board from closing and binding the saw blade.

On a table saw, reduce the chance of kickback during ripping by using a feather board ahead of the blade. To keep your hands away from the blade, feed the board with a push stick. Never reach over the blade.

A circular saw can rip even a large sheet of plywood accurately if you use a long straightedge *(pages 18–19)* securely clamped to the wood. Place supports under the sheet as shown.

Safely cutting large sheets of plywood on a table saw requires a second pair of hands. The helper holds the sheet level without lifting or pulling as you feed the other end through the blade.

Crosscutting

With a portable circular saw: First support the wood on both sides of the cut. Then tightly clamp a piece of scrapwood to the workpiece along the cut line to act as a saw guide. Hold the board firmly as you make the cut.

On a table saw: Use the saw's miter gauge, which rides in a slot as it carries the board through the blade, not the rip fence. For even greater accuracy, lengthen the face of the miter gauge by fastening a piece of square, true scrapwood to its face.

With a handsaw: Clamp a piece of scrapwood on the cut line as a blade guide. For a smooth cut, use long, even strokes and gentle pressure, not short, fast, jerky strokes that can leave you with a rough cut— or, even worse, a bent and ruined saw.

RIP RIGHT
Know which side is up

The tiny splinters, fractures, and rough edges caused by a blade exiting the wood is called tear-out. This is especially noticeable when ripping plywood with power saws.

To avoid tear-out when using a portable circular saw, place the best face of the workpiece *down* and away from the blade when ripping. Any tear-out will then occur on the bad side of the sheet, which will probably be hidden. For that reason, draw all cut lines on the bad face.

When ripping with a table saw, do just the opposite. Draw cut lines on the best face and place that side *up* on the table.

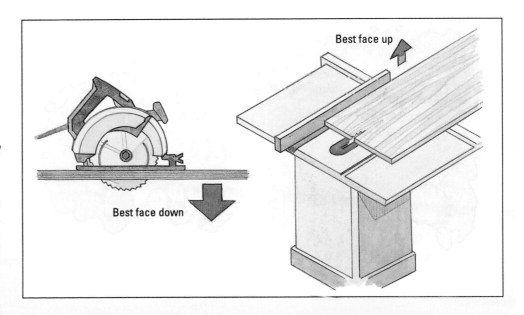

Best face up

Best face down

ANGLED AND CURVED CUTS

Rips and crosscuts separate materials. Angled cuts are used primarily in the early stages of rejoining materials. Curved cuts shape wood decoratively.

A miter is probably the most common type of angle cut. They're usually made at 45 degrees in order to join two pieces of wood at a 90-degree angle *(page 47)*, as in a picture frame. Cutting an accurate miter is more difficult than it looks because even the slightest movement of the wood or shifting of the cutting tool will throw it off.

Bevels are cuts of more or less than 45 degrees. They're made on the edges and/or ends of boards, mostly for decorative reasons. Use a tool called a T-bevel to record and transfer unusual angles.

Curved cuts in wood also add a decorative element. When used to join moldings in corners, they're called "copes."

Miter cuts

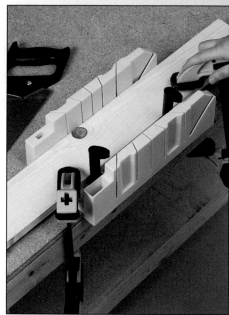

1 Use a miter box. Mark the cut line, place the workpiece in the box and align the cut line with the corresponding notches. Clamp the piece flush with the edge of the miter box that's farthest from you as you saw.

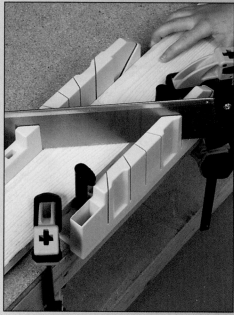

2 Make the cut with smooth, even strokes. Get the cut started with a couple of pull strokes, then use gentle, even pressure and cut on the forward stroke. Keep the saw level, especially when finishing the cut, or you'll saw through the floor of the miter box.

With a portable circular saw, clamp the workpiece in place, draw a cut line, then hold a saw guide next to the saw's bottom plate to steady the saw.

On a table saw, short miters are made with the help of the miter gauge. Set the gauge, place the wood against its fence, then feed the stock smoothly through the blade using the miter slot.

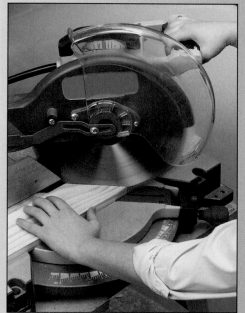

With a power miter saw, set the degree angle of the saw, position the board, and make the cut. A compound miter saw allows you to tilt the saw head as well as angle it.

Beveled cuts

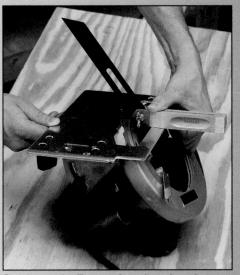

Record the angle: At times you have to cut a bevel on a workpiece to match an existing angle. Rather than calculating it, record the old angle with a sliding bevel that adjusts and locks by turning a wing nut. You can use it to transfer both inside and outside angles.

Set the angle: To transfer a bevel angle to a portable circular saw, unplug the tool and turn it over. Loosen the foot plate, and with the bevel in place, tilt the foot plate to the desired angle, then retighten it. Ensure the blade depth will cut through the material.

On a table saw: Use a similar technique to transfer an angle with the sliding bevel to a table saw. Loosen the arbor lock, place the bevel against the blade, and turn the tilt wheel until the angle of the blade aligns with that of the sliding bevel.

Curved cuts

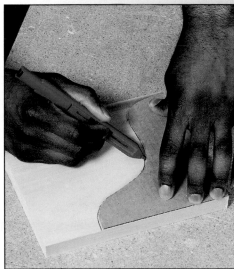

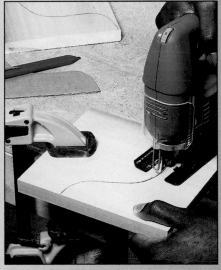

1 A jigsaw easily follows curved and rounded pattern lines for scrolling cuts. If you have a pattern to follow, trace it onto a piece of cardboard, then cut it out to make a template. Use the template to transfer the pattern to the wood by drawing a cut line with a pencil.

2 Clamp the workpiece securely to your workbench, making sure the saw's blade won't cut into supporting surfaces. Sometimes you need to make a partial cut, then reposition the workpiece and reclamp it before continuing to make the cut.

Need to cut a pair?

Cutting exact duplicates is fast and easy if you use masking tape to join the workpieces. Mark the cut on one piece, then apply the tape to tightly join the pieces in precise alignment. It doesn't matter where you place the tape, as the saw will cut right through it, but don't hide the pattern line. You also can use double-faced carpet tape, which you apply in between the two pieces.

DRILLING

Making holes in wood requires two basic tools: a bit to cut and a driver to propel it. If you want the hole to be of a precise depth or angle, you'll need some extra help.

Although you can use a hand-powered brace or a hand drill, a corded electric drill or a cordless drill/driver gives you better control and more power at comparatively little added cost. An accessory drill guide greatly increases accuracy.

Available bits number in the hundreds. For woodworking, though, avoid the standard twist drill bit. Its shallowly beveled point is designed to penetrate metal, but unless carefully controlled, it tends to wander on wood. Instead use brad-point bits. These have a sharp center point that keeps the hole where you want it. Tapered drills and countersink bits enable you to make pilot and countersink holes for the screws shown below. A drill stop limits hole depth.

As you go through this book, you'll see other special drilling accessories described that will help make your work easier and more accurate.

Drilling repetitive holes, such as those needed for a bookcase's adjustable shelves, is accurately done by using a piece of pegboard as a spacing template.

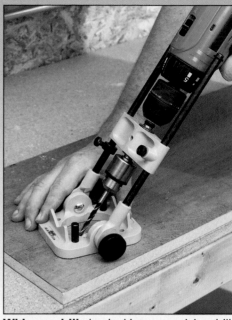

With your drill chucked into a precision drill guide, you can accurately drill at any angle between 45 and 90 degrees. The guide's built-in depth stop limits hole depth.

Drilling horizontal holes

To drill straight holes—not angled ones—horizontally, slip a metal washer over the bit as a guide. The washer should be a close fit on the shaft. If the drill is perpendicular when the bit is turning, the washer won't walk along the bit.

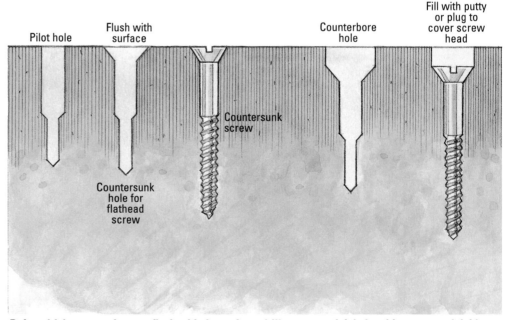

Before driving a wood screw flush with the surface, drill a countersink hole with a countersink bit. Use a combination bit to drill a countersink hole with a counterbore in which to recess the screw. Conceal the screw head with a standard wood plug or one you made with a plug-cutting bit.

CHISELING

One of a woodworker's simplest tools is a chisel. For general use, a blade that's 3–5 inches long will do. But you'll likely end up with several chisels of differing lengths and widths. Buy chisels that have high-carbon steel blades and durable handles (plastic handles absorb shock and resist deformation when hit with a mallet). Use a dead blow hammer or wood mallet to drive a chisel.

Chisels are versatile tools. They perform many woodworking tasks well—if you keep them sharp and handle them carefully and properly. Don't use them to pry open paint cans or stuck windows, and they'll give you years of good service.

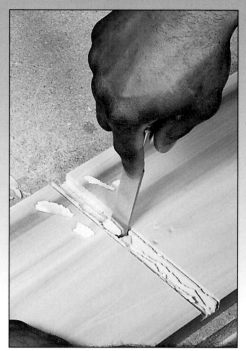

1 Clean out a dado or groove cut with a saw by turning the chisel bevel down to pare away the small ridges. Don't pry, cut.

2 Finish cleaning groove by turning the chisel bevel up and running it through the groove or dado to flatten and smooth the bottom.

STANLEY. PRO TIP

Choosing a chisel

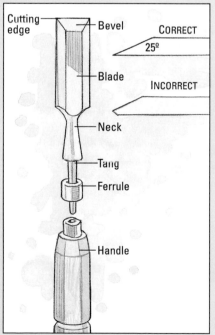

A good wood-handled chisel has a steel hoop at the top of the handle to keep it from mushrooming. Plastic handles absorb shock.

KEEP CHISELS SHARP
How to hone on a flat stone

1 Start with the stone's coarser side up; apply a light coat of oil to the stone. With firm, even pressure, move the chisel's bevel side around the stone in a figure-eight pattern. Make sure both the heel and toe of the bevel remain in contact with stone.

2 A thin piece of excess metal will develop at the tip, called a "wire edge." To remove it, turn over the chisel, lay it flat on the stone, and give it a few light sideways strokes. Turn over the stone and repeat the steps on the finer-grained side.

PUTTING IT ALL TOGETHER

The process of assembling a project's wooden parts and subassemblies is called joinery. It's among the most complex aspects of woodworking and demands a thorough understanding of the properties of wood and precision craftsmanship. It is also among the most rewarding processes, turning a collection of what looks like miscellaneous pieces of wood into a sturdy and attractive piece of furniture. The stronger and more durable the joint, the more demanding the work will be. That's why woodworkers decide early on what joints they'll use. In this chapter, you'll learn how to make many traditional joints, as well as some new, faster, easier ways woodworkers have come up with to make strong joints. You'll find that even the more complex joints can be mastered if you work carefully and methodically and understand wood movement and grain direction.

Wood movement

Wood is a hygroscopic material: it has the ability to absorb moisture and swell, as well as discharge it and shrink, even when covered with finish. That's why a drawer that slides easily in winter at low humidity may stick in summer when humidity is high. This tendency for wood to change dimension—even if only minutely—is called wood movement.

Joinery techniques take wood movement into consideration by withstanding it, allowing it, or placing pieces so movement has little effect on the joint.

Grain direction

When you look at the end of a board, you'll see a pattern in the wood that's quite different from what's on its edge, face or back. Softwoods show a series of separated lines representing the tree's growth layers. In hardwoods, depending on their density, you may see a similar pattern, simply a series of minuscule pores, or a combination of both. It's all end grain, and it all wicks up moisture—as you'll notice when applying finish.

That's why it's best to avoid end-grain-to-end-grain joints. The glue disappears into the wood, leaving little or nothing to permanently bond the pieces together. Without additional strengthening, such as dowels, an end-grain-to-end-grain joint eventually comes apart.

Creating tight, strong joints is one of the most demanding, but rewarding tasks in woodworking.

CHAPTER PREVIEW

Basic joints
page 46

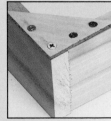
Reinforced joints
page 51

Advanced joints
page 52

Clamping
page 53

Clamps and glue are the last stages in joinery. It's the careful planning and precision cutting and fitting preceding glue-up that ensures a sturdy and elegant piece. Here C-clamps and bar clamps—carefully buffered with pieces of scrapwood so as not to mar the finished piece—aid in the final assembly of a mitered corner.

BASIC JOINTS

Edge joints create a panel from several narrow boards. The result is stronger and more resistant to splitting and warping than a single wide piece of wood.

A **butt joint** joins two pieces at 90 degrees in a corner or along the pieces' length. Reinforce these joints for strength.

Cutting away part of two pieces to be joined adds gluing surface and creates lap joints. For a **half-lap joint,** remove half of each piece's thickness. In a lap joint, material is removed only from one piece.

A **miter joint** demands an accurate 45-degree cut on both pieces to be joined. Add strength to these joints with glue blocks or screws.

Edge joint

1 With all edges perfectly square, lay the boards on equally spaced bar clamps. Adjust them for visual appeal, then mark with a pencil for later realignment.

2 Turn all but the first board on edge. Apply a thin, even coat of woodworking glue to one of each mating edge with a small brush. Be sure board edges are completely coated.

3 Align boards on the bottom clamps. Place scrapwood between the clamps and workpiece. Tighten clamps. Turn over the workpiece and repeat. Leave clamped until glue dries.

Half-lap joint

1 Mark the edges for cuts as you hold the two boards together. Measure for width and thickness. The depth of the cut is the thickness of the thinner piece.

2 With the help of a try or combination square, draw the width and depth cut lines onto the thicker of the two pieces.

3 Using a backsaw, make the first cut across the grain to the depth indicated by the mark. Hold the saw at 90 degrees to the wood as you cut.

4 Make the final cut through the end grain to remove the waste. Either turn the wood on edge and saw vertically or stand the wood on end in a vise.

Butt joint

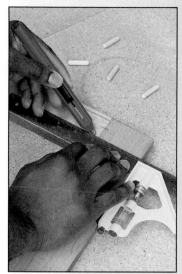 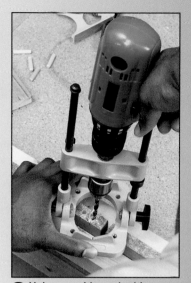  

1 Strengthen a visible butt joint with dowels. Begin by marking the location of each dowel's center, about 1½ inches apart, on one of the pieces to be joined.

2 Using a guide and a bit that's the same size as your dowels, drill holes slightly longer than one-half the dowel length into the center of one piece at the dowel markings.

3 Dowel centers mark the exact location of the dowel holes in the second piece. Insert one (of your dowel size) in each hole, then press the two pieces to be joined together to mark.

4 Drop glue into each dowel hole. Spread glue around half the length of each dowel. Tap each halfway into its hole. Glue holes and exposed dowels, then draw together.

Miter joint

 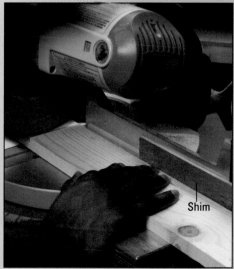 

Shim

With a miter box: A power miter saw provides great accuracy, but with care, mitering can be done with a backsaw and miter box. With either, mark the 45-degree cut line, then hold or clamp the piece while sawing.

Corrections: After sawing both pieces to 45 degrees, fit them together to check the angle. If the cut was slightly awry, correct it by placing a tiny shim against the fence or inside the miter box, then resaw.

Clamping: A miter clamp holds the two joined pieces together while the glue dries. It also keeps the pieces joined if you want to strengthen the joint with brads or finishing nails after the glue dries.

Dado joint

1 Dadoes are channels that run across the grain. They're often used in the sides of a bookcase to hold shelves. Use a carpenter's square and pencil to mark their location and widths on the wood. If the project uses plywood shelves, double-check their thickness. Don't assume ¾-inch plywood will always be ¾ inch thick. Dimensions vary with the manufacturer, and if the dadoes are not the exact width of the shelves' thickness, you'll have a bad fit.

2 Cutting a dado with a portable circular saw requires setting the blade to the depth you want the dado, usually one-third the wood's thickness. (Be sure the blade is perpendicular to the saw's foot plate.) Next, with a straightedge as a guide, saw kerfs in the wood to shape the dado edges. Then saw narrowly spaced kerfs in the wood remaining between the sides.

RABBET AND DADO JOINTS

Shoulder

Double rabbet

Rabbet

Through dado joint

3 Short dadoes can be cut with a backsaw. Clamp a piece of wood with one true edge to the saw as a depth gauge. Then make multiple, thinly spaced cuts to dado width.

4 To clean waste out of the dado, move a chisel from side to side with the bevel pointing down. Then run the chisel (bevel side up) down the dado's length. This flattens and smooths the bottom of the dado.

Rabbet joint

1 Rabbets are cut in one end or along the length of a board or panel to accept and support another piece of wood. They are usually the width of that piece and up to one-half the workpiece's depth. Use a depth gauge to mark the rabbet's width.

2 On a table saw, cut the rabbet's width (shoulder cut) with the workpiece flat on the table and against the rip fence. Set the blade to desired depth, turn the board on edge and against the fence, and run it through the saw.

3 A router cuts small rabbets in one pass, larger and deeper ones in a few shallow passes. Chuck a piloted rabbeting bit of the correct size and set to desired depth of cut. Securely clamp the workpiece to your bench top while routing the rabbet.

Groove joint

1 Grooves run with the grain and away from the edge. Use a straight-cutting bit and either the router's edge guide or a clamped straightedge as a guide. For deep grooves, make several shallow passes.

2 As with dadoes, you can cut grooves with a handsaw too. You'll need a longer straightedge that you'll have to move several times as you cut kerfs across the groove's width. Chisel out waste.

STANLEY PRO TIP

Labels help you avoid costly errors

When you're working with expensive hardwoods or hardwood plywood, you don't want to make a mistake. To prevent accidentally sawing a dado, rabbet, or groove in the wrong side of a workpiece, use masking tape to label where cuts will go. It's easily removed, and you can wipe off any remaining adhesive with a solvent.

Mortise-and-tenon joint

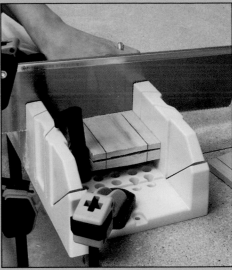

1 Measure and mark for a tenon's length and shoulders on the end and all four sides of the stock, using a combination or try square. Make the tenon from one-third to one-half the stock's thickness and about $\frac{1}{16}$ inch shorter than the mortise's depth. In a through mortise, the tenon should be $\frac{1}{8}$ inch longer than the stock thickness of the mortised piece.

2 Tightly clamp the marked tenon piece in a bench vise, using scrapwood to protect the sides of the workpiece from the clamp jaws. With a backsaw, carefully saw through the end grain to the shoulder line on either side of the tenon. Take care to keep the saw perpendicular to the wood. For a four-shouldered tenon, make two more cuts down the narrow sides.

3 To complete the tenon, remove the workpiece from the vise and securely clamp it in your miter box with a waste side up. Use a backsaw guided by the miter box slots to free the waste from one of the tenon sides. With that cut complete, turn over the workpiece and repeat. If the tenon will have four shoulders, turn the workpiece on edge to make those cuts.

4 Use the tenon as a pattern to mark the outline of the mortise on the mating workpiece. Center the tenoned piece on the stock to be mortised. A blind mortise requires marking only one side. For a through mortise, carefully transfer position lines to the other side and mark.

5 You can cut a mortise with a mortising chisel, but an electric drill is faster. Using a bit about the same diameter as the mortise width and a drill stop, drill overlapping holes to remove most of the waste. For a through mortise, place scrapwood under the workpiece to prevent splintering.

6 After drilling, clean up the sides of the mortise with a sharp chisel. Keep the chisel's bevel facing the mortise. Be particular about the mortise corners; they must be smooth and square. With a through mortise, turn over the workpiece and use the chisel to clean up the other side too.

REINFORCED JOINTS

Some of the simplest joints to make need help when asked to do heftier jobs than they were designed to do. A glued miter joint *(page 47)* holds up well in a picture frame, but if used in building a cabinet door or face frame, it won't stand up without increasing its strength with wood **dowels.** Miter joints reinforced with dowels hold better than glue alone, and they add visual appeal.

Many simple joints used to build utility shelving or casework benefit from equally simple reinforcement. Turn to metal **plates** and **brackets** from the home center or hardware store, or make your own **plywood gussets** and wooden **corner blocks.**

Even traditionally strong joints like the mortise-and-tenon benefit from a peg that locks the two parts together.

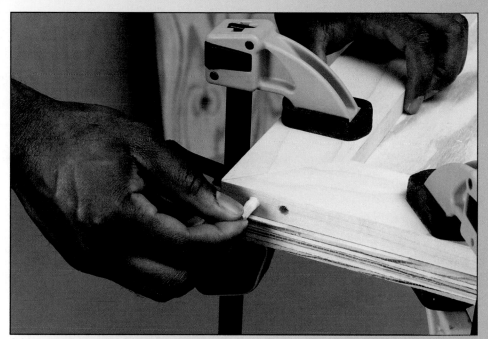

Add strength to a miter joint by adding dowels. Glue and clamp the joint first and let dry. Drill dowel holes deep enough to penetrate both the joined pieces. Apply glue to the dowels and insert them into the holes, tapping as necessary. Saw off any protruding dowels and sand them flush.

Wood and metal gusset and strap

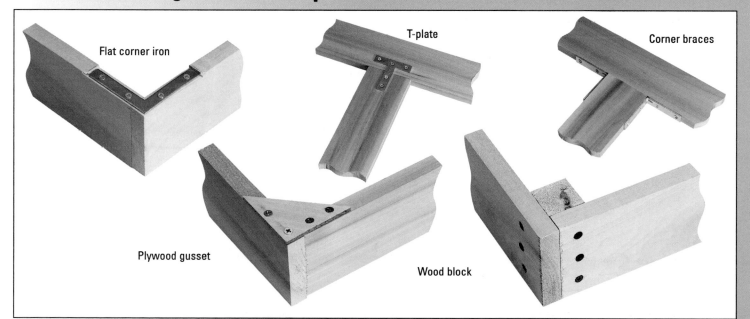

Flat corner iron

T-plate

Corner braces

Plywood gusset

Wood block

Metal and wood reinforcements for simple joints are normally placed where they're less visible—at the back of a bookcase or inside a cabinet, for instance. You might also think of these strengtheners when it's time to shore up old bookcases and other furniture. Each of them takes only minutes to install.

ADVANCED JOINTS

Done right, traditional joinery takes a lot of time. That's why woodworkers seek quicker ways to accomplish the same result. During the past decade, two new joinery techniques have grown in popularity.

Pocket-hole joinery employs a small, fairly inexpensive jig; a special bit; and auger-point screws to cut project construction time in half. The technique is easy to use and eliminates the need for a shop filled with clamps.

Biscuit joinery uses a biscuit or plate joiner to cut oval-shape slots in the wood pieces. Compressed wood biscuits are inserted in the slots and glued. The glue makes the biscuits expand, creating a solid joint.

Pocket-hole joinery

Pocket-hole jig

Reinforcing block

1 To assemble, clamp the pocket-hole jig in place. Set the depth stop; then, guided by the jig, drill angled screw holes in one of the pieces.

2 After drilling the holes, remove the jig from the workpiece. Apply glue to the mating piece and butt the two together. Drive the screws.

3 Pocket-hole joinery, best used where it won't be visible, makes it easy to attach reinforcing corner blocks to a project.

Biscuit joinery

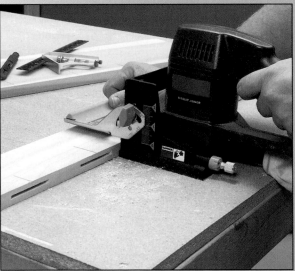

1 Use a speed square or combination square to mark biscuit locations in both boards. The boards must be machined as for edge joining *(page 46)*.

2 Clamp the workpiece in place and center the biscuit joiner on a mark. Cut out the biscuit slot, then repeat for all slots in each board.

3 Insert biscuits without glue in the edge of one board and test fit. Make any needed adjustments. When you're satisfied with the fit, apply glue evenly inside the slots on both pieces and to all mating surfaces. Clamp and let dry.

CLAMPING

Clamping is as important to sound joinery as machining and glue are. Glue alone will hold two pieces of wood together, but a good bond requires pressure to force the glue into the wood's fibers. Clamping also holds a project's parts in proper position until the glue dries and anchors them.

Walk the tool aisle in a home center and you'll discover dozens of clamp types in myriad sizes. You won't need them all, but you should have the essentials shown here.

For large projects like bookcases and cabinets, **bar clamps** or **pipe clamps** are indispensable. Special purpose clamps, such as the **band clamp,** even binds cylinders. For holding small assemblies together, **spring clamps** always come in handy.

Many more types of specialty clamps can be found. Remember, as with all tools beyond the basics, buy clamps only as you need them.

Pipe clamps hold large assemblies, such as this bookcase, together while glue dries. Note the wood strips under the clamp jaws at top and bottom. These "cauls" distribute clamp pressure.

Bar clamps do the same work as pipe clamps. Note how the clamps on this cabinet face frame are placed at the joints most likely to need support. Bar clamps can be laid flat on a surface.

STANLEY PRO TIP

Checking for square

There's nothing more frustrating than finding that a case is out of square *after* the glue has dried. Check for square before the glue sets by measuring diagonally from corner to corner, first one way, then the other. When measurements are equal, the case is square. If not, adjust and reset the clamps.

A band clamp holds together boxes and odd-shaped projects while you reinforce joints or make repairs, such as to a shaky drawer. They are not meant for use with large projects.

Spring clamps work well in pairs or in a series for small joinery work. They are easier to adjust and tighten than the standard C-clamp, and they have a protective rubber coating that won't mar wood surfaces.

FINISHING TOUCHES

The project is finally built. You chose the perfect design, the best material and hardware, and put it all together with some outstanding joinery. Now it's ready for finish.

Or almost ready. Careful preparation is the difference between a ho-hum finish and one you'll love to touch and admire. In this chapter, you'll learn how to properly prepare your project for finishing, select the right finish for the job, and apply it like a pro. We'll guide you through the final steps of crafting a project you're proud to show off.

The need to finish

Finishes primarily protect wood and wood products from absorbing or expelling moisture too fast, which can lead to warping, cracking, and loose joints. Finishes also add protection from dirt, oxidation, spills, and stains. They aid in cleaning, allowing you to wipe off dirt and moisture that would otherwise penetrate and permanently stain the wood.

Finishes make wood projects more beautiful, too. Clear finishes allow you to actually see down into the wood, making a rich grain sparkle. Stains can change a wood's color and bring out contrast in the grain patterns. Some stains make inexpensive wood look more like an exotic species. Paint can give your projects a colorful gloss or a rich glow. It also conceals plywood edges, fasteners, and puttied-over dings, dents, scratches, and other imperfections.

Where to finish

Because preparation creates dust and finishing produces odors, wear protective safety equipment (page 15), and set aside a special place for these tasks.

If you have a shop, you can do most of your finish preparation at your workbench, including dust-producing activities such as sanding. But it's a good idea to clean a special area just for finish application and drying, so dust and dirt won't mar your results. Or designate a room or part of the basement (not where the furnace or water heater are, as dust and finish fumes can be flammable or explosive) or garage for it. Be sure you have good ventilation and bright lighting. Sometimes, weather permitting, finishing (especially preparation) is done outdoors.

A poor finish results from second-rate preparation. Take the time to do it right.

CHAPTER PREVIEW

Preparing wood
page 56

Paints, stains, and finishes
page 58

Applying finishes
page 60

Finishes do more than enhance the beauty of wood. They slow the wood's ability to absorb moisture and protect wood from scratches, stains, and dirt. Obtaining a beautiful finish requires some preparation; don't rush the process.

PREPARING WOOD

Pave the way for a great finish by getting the wood as smooth and perfect as possible. That means finding and filling defects, concealing unsightly edges in plywood, and sanding thoroughly.

Detecting defects

Natural defects in wood include tiny, solid knots; thin splits or cracks; and minuscule pest holes. Inspect your project carefully for these and note them. If you find them in hardwood that you plan to apply a stain and clear finish to, it's best to wait until after you've completed the finishing to attend to them. Then use a colored putty that matches the final finish.

On the other hand, fill small gaps and other minuscule imperfections prior to adding a clear finish. One way to do this is to mix some of the wood's sawdust (the finer the better; the dust-collecting bag or cup of a finishing sander, if yours is so equipped, is a great source) with a bit of the finish and fill with that. The other way is to simply buy a prepared filler in a matching color.

Treat the rough edges of softwood plywood you plan to paint with a commercial filler (or exterior spackling compound). Then sand the repair. For hardwood plywood, use iron-on veneer tape of the same wood species. In some cases, moldings *(page 33)* can conceal as well as add eye appeal.

Sand smooth

Do all prefinish sanding with orange-colored, open-coat garnet sandpaper. Dust won't clog it as easily as closed-coat papers, so it lasts longer and works better. For hand-sanding, "A" weight paper works best. Wrap it around a sanding block so the surface you're working on remains flat as you smooth it.

The higher the grit number, the finer the grit. For most work, start with 100 grit, then use 150, and end with 220 grit. Clean the surface of the wood between sandings with a vacuum, a tack cloth, or a paper towel lightly dampened with a solvent such as lacquer thinner.

Filling

1 Use a nail set and a hammer to drive the nailhead below the wood surface. Press filler in the hole, let it dry, then sand flush.

2 Softwood and softwood plywood often have blemishes that will telegraph through a finish. To prevent this, apply a wood filler with a putty knife, then sand when dry.

Edges

Wood filler: Softwood plywood edges usually have a rough look. If you decide to paint the wood, spread wood filler in the voids and sand smooth when dry. Exterior spackling compound also works well.

Veneer tape: Easily applied, heat-activated veneer tape neatly covers hardwood plywood edges. Simply trim it with a crafts knife, and use an iron set on medium-low to adhere the tape.

Sanding

A belt sander quickly smooths large surfaces, such as plywood sheets. It is aggressive, however, so keep it moving. If held too long in one place, it can dig into the wood and cause a low spot.

Orbital finishing sanders do a fine job on hardwoods and are lightweight and maneuverable. They are handy for small areas and narrow parts.

A sanding block produces the best results when hand-sanding. Purchase one or make one from a piece of scrapwood. Change paper frequently.

The right abrasive

Select the correct grit for the woodworking job at hand.

Grit	Uses
36–80	Surfacing rough wood
60–100	Rough sanding saw marks
120–320	Smooth sanding
80–320	Sanding contours
240–600	Sanding between coats

Open-coat papers in garnet or aluminum oxide are preferred.

STANLEY PRO TIP: **Dampen hardwood for final sanding**

Get a super-smooth surface on hardwoods by dampening them before the final sanding. Simply moisten a lint-free cloth and wipe down the wood. This raises the "hairs" in the grain so you can remove them with fine sandpaper for a silk-smooth surface.

PAINTS, STAINS, AND FINISHES

The chart on the next page tells you what to expect from several types of finishes. The photo above it shows what some popular finishes look like when they're applied to commonly used materials. Here are the basic differences between finish categories:

Paint completely obscures the material it covers and is the easiest to apply. Its colored pigments are suspended in either water (water-based/latex paint) or a petroleum product (oil-based paint). Water is the solvent for the first; and paint thinner or mineral spirits is the solvent for the latter. Paint is available in three levels of sheen: flat (little sheen), semigloss (medium sheen), and high-gloss (high sheen). Generally you use paint to coat less expensive materials.

Stain colors wood too, but the thin pigment highlights and emphasizes grain features instead of hiding them. Both water-based and oil-based stains are simple to apply but must be followed by a clear top coat. (You also can thin paint for use as a stain.)

Clear finishes come in water-based and oil-based varieties, as different types of oils (penetrating), and in combinations. These finishes maximize wood's features and usually add a slight, warm color. The hardest to apply without fault, they normally require several coats for the best appearance and protection.

What to have on hand

You won't need all the items pictured below for each type of finish. Applicators, for instance, differ with the type of finish you select. The personnel in the finishing department at a home center or hardware store can advise you on your specific needs. **Brushes** are either foam, synthetic bristle, or natural bristle. Natural bristle works best when applying oil-based products. You can use a **roller** with either water- or oil-based coatings, but it will add texture. Lint-free **cheesecloth** is an optional applicator for stains and clear finishing oils.

Steel wool in the fine (#000) and finest (#0000) grades levels a finish between coats. Don't use it with water-based finishes— any residue will rust! Woven **abrasive pads** perform like steel wool with all finishes.

Fill sticks repair minor surface imperfections, while **wood filler** handles larger ones *(see page 56)*. **Putty knives** are valuable when filling large surface defects.

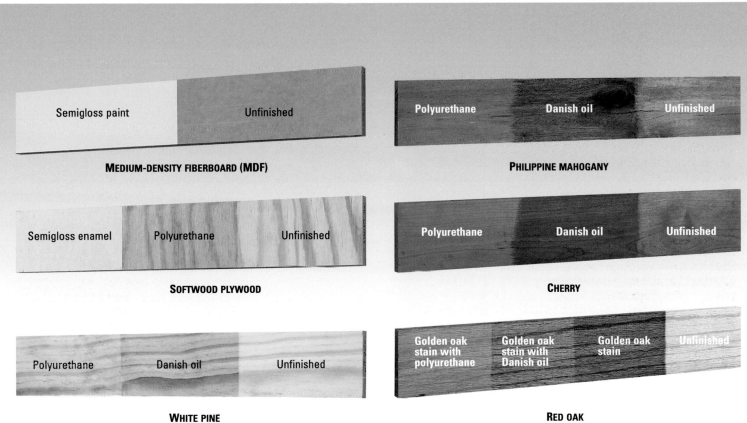

MEDIUM-DENSITY FIBERBOARD (MDF)

Semigloss paint | Unfinished

PHILIPPINE MAHOGANY

Polyurethane | Danish oil | Unfinished

SOFTWOOD PLYWOOD

Semigloss enamel | Polyurethane | Unfinished

CHERRY

Polyurethane | Danish oil | Unfinished

WHITE PINE

Polyurethane | Danish oil | Unfinished

RED OAK

Golden oak stain with polyurethane | Golden oak stain with Danish oil | Golden oak stain | Unfinished

FINISH FEATURES

Not all finishes perform or apply equally. Note the comments following each type to aid in your selection. Finishes described are normally available at home centers and hardware stores.

Type of finish	Description	Application	Comments
PAINT			
Water-based	Easy to apply, simple cleanup	Synthetic brush, roller	Endless colors, two coats, fast drying
Oil-based	Easy to apply, durable	Natural bristle brush, roller	Bad odor, flammable, slow drying
CLEAR SURFACE FINISHES			
Lacquer	Moderately durable, lustrous	Best sprayed	Many coats, flammable, bad odor, fast drying
Varnish	Durable, clear	Natural bristle brush	Flammable, bad odor, slow drying, yellows
Polyurethane varnish	High durability/protection	Natural/synthetic/foam brush	Flammable, bad odor, slow drying
Water-based varnish	Durable, no color, easy cleanup	Synthetic/foam brush, spray	Nonflammable, fast drying
Shellac	Easy to apply, hard cleanup	Natural bristle brush	Low protection, needs wax, many coats, flammable
PENETRATING FINISHES			
Danish oil	Easy to apply, enhances grain	Natural bristle brush/cloth	Low protection, many coats, slow drying
Tung oil	Easy to apply, low luster	Natural bristle brush/cloth	Low protection, many coats, slow drying

APPLYING FINISHES

Apply stain with either a brush or a cloth, always in the direction of the grain. It may look muddy at first—that's why you wipe it off with a cloth before it dries. The remaining pigment soaks into the wood pores, giving it color. If it's too light, repeat the steps. For a lighter color, limit a stain's penetration by first sealing the wood with a prepared "wood conditioner" or a thinned coat of clear finish.

When you apply any clear finish to wood, start at one edge of the piece and work in the direction of the grain. Smooth out any ridges and pools in the finish while it's still wet with cross-grain strokes. Some finishes, such as water-based varnish and shellac, dry quickly, making this hard to do.

For greater visual appeal and durability, apply multiple coats of clear finishes, rubbing with #0000 steel wool or very fine abrasive between each coat.

Stain

1 Mix stain thoroughly before using. With either a brush or lint-free cloth, apply it in the direction of the grain. Overlap your strokes slightly so you don't miss any spots.

2 Before the stain begins to dry, wipe the entire wood surface to remove excess. This also forces the stain's pigment into the grain, enhancing contrast.

Penetrating oil

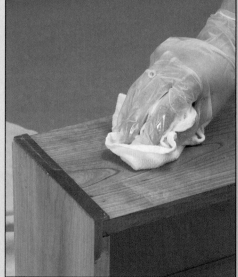

1 When using any type of penetrating oil finish, flood a liberal amount onto the wood, then spread it around with a lint-free cloth. For large areas, do a section at a time.

2 Let the oil soak in for about 10 minutes (read label directions). Wipe to remove excess oil. Allow the finish to dry 24 hours before applying a second coat. Reapply until the wood will not absorb any more oil.

3 For a satiny-smooth oil finish, rub the dry surface between coats with extra-fine (#0000) steel wool. Wipe off the entire surface after rubbing. When the oil has cured, apply paste wax for protection.

Clear surface finish

1 Stir, don't shake, the polyurethane. For the smoothest application, use a disposable foam brush and work across the grain to fill the pores.

2 For the second coat, brush with the grain so any ridges of finish won't be as visible. To avoid runs, don't load the brush when working near edges.

3 When the finish has thoroughly dried, go over it with #0000 steel wool or fine (320-grit) abrasive. Repeat between coats.

4 Small flaws such as nicks and nail holes can be filled with a tinted filler stick of matching color after the finish has completely dried.

Paint

1 A first coat of sanding sealer, then a second of primer helps ensure a smooth final paint coat. Sand it lightly with fine abrasive.

2 Fill any defects that show up in the primer coat—even tiny flaws—with spackling compound or wood filler.

3 After filling, go over the entire project with a finish sander and extra-fine abrasive. Grain direction doesn't matter.

4 Thoroughly clean off the sanding dust with a vacuum or tack cloth. Stir paint, then brush on evenly with the grain.

Easy, Great-Looking Shelves You Can Build

No other home furnishing offers the variety and versatility that shelves do. They can be simple or ornate. They can be constructed of rough, unfinished materials or fine hardwoods that have been carefully machined and coated with a lustrous finish. They can serve to store or display, organize or catch clutter.

This chapter presents five shelf designs, from a simple wall-mounted display shelf to a furniture-quality shelf stand in the Mission style. You'll find instructions for building expandable utility shelving for your basement or garage; dramatic "floating" display shelves; and smart-looking modular boxes that stack. Each project is easy to build, with complete construction plans, a materials list, and step-by-step instructions.

Any of the projects can be completed by a novice do-it-yourselfer using the tools and skills presented in the preceding chapters. The display shelf is the easiest to complete; the Mission-style stand is the most involved.

Material options

All the shelf designs incorporate materials that are available at home centers or lumberyards. Most use nominal-size boards—such as 1×2 or 1×4—that need to be cut only to length before assembly.

The instructions for each project specify the type of material to use, but keep in mind that you can build them with materials of your choice. For example, the floating shelves on *page 68* are shown made from oak, with a stain and clear finish, but you may choose to construct them of pine and paint them. The modular boxes on *page 72* could be made of medium-density fiberboard (MDF). It's less expensive than the birch plywood shown but doesn't take a finish as well.

Trim options abound too. For example, you may find a specification for colonial base molding, but if there's another molding profile that matches your decor, or one that you simply like better, use it. Substituting another style won't alter the project's basic construction. And after all, customizing a project to your taste and decorative style is the satisfying and fun part of building something yourself. So when you're looking at a project, imagine how you want it to appear in your home.

Shelves can add more than storage to your home.

CHAPTER PREVIEW

Display shelf
page 64

Floating shelves
page 68

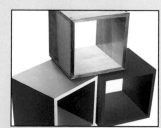

Modular boxes
page 72

Mission-style utility stand
page 76

Utility shelves
page 84

The "floating" display shelves (page 68) make use of ready-made molding pieces to add flair to their simple design. The project demands only basic woodworking skills: accurate measuring and cutting, drilling holes, hammering nails, and driving screws.
Read the preceding chapters on tools, materials, and skills before launching any of the projects in the rest of the book.

DISPLAY SHELF

Hang this simple shelf in your bedroom, bath, entryway, kitchen, or living room. Its clean lines enhance whatever you choose to display on it. Those same lines are your clue that this project is easy to build from materials readily available at home centers.

Size considerations
At 32 inches long, the shelf is sized to span two wall studs spaced 16 inches on center (OC), the traditional construction of a framed plaster or drywall-covered wall. If you want to lengthen it, keep stud spacing in mind. Some homes are built using 24-inch stud spacing. If your walls are lath-and-plaster or brick, you'll need to use appropriate hangers *(page 71)*.

Other treatments
Although this shelf is shown in naturally finished maple, it can easily be made of another wood, such as walnut or pine. Finish options are as wide as the variety of stains and paints available *(page 59)*. Keep in mind, though, that less expensive woods, such as pine, look best when painted.

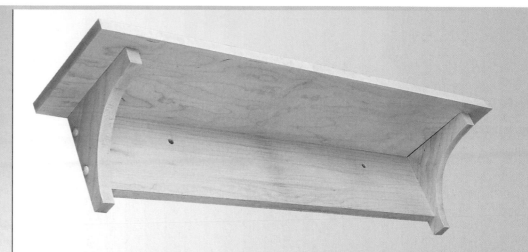

Build one or several of this design in an afternoon or evening. Mounted directly to wall studs, it can display heavy objects.

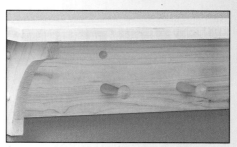

As an option, add ready-made maple Shaker pegs to hang hats and coats.

If you like, cut a groove in the shelf top to display a collection of plates.

PRESTART CHECKLIST

☐ **TIME**
About two hours to construct, plus an hour to finish

☐ **TOOLS**
Tape measure, clamps, drill bits, counterbore, countersink, electric drill/driver, circular saw or table saw, jigsaw with hardwood cutting blade, combination square, level, stud finder

☐ **SKILLS**
Sawing, gluing, clamping

☐ **PREP**
Find and mark wall studs at shelf location

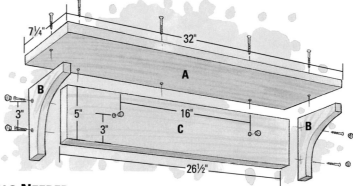

MATERIALS NEEDED

Part	Finished size			Mat.	Qty.
	T	W	L		
A top shelf	¾"	7¼"	32"	HM	1
B supports	¾"	6¼"	6"	HM	2
C support rail	¾"	5"	26½"	HM	1

Material key: HM–hard maple
Hardware: #8×3", #8×1½" FHWS
Supplies: Glue, ⅜" maple mushroom screw hole plugs, ⅜" maple screw hole plugs, sandpaper, clear finish

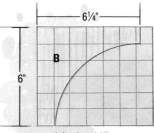

1-inch grid squares

A. Forming parts

1 Cut the top (A) to size and check the ends for square. Measure and mark the points where you'll drill the screws through the top to attach the support rail (C) and the side supports (B).

2 Copy the side support pattern grid *(page 64)* onto heavy paper (each square = 1 inch). Make pencil dots where the pattern line crosses the grid lines. Connect the dots to form an arc.

Grain of board

45º

3 Place the cutout pattern on a maple piece wide enough for the support. With a combination square, draw a line at a 45-degree angle to the wood's grain direction. Align the pattern with the line and trace it onto the board. Repeat for a second piece (two are needed).

STANLEY PRO TIP

Break the edges

Sharp saw blades leave sharp edges on wood that can cut and tear your hands. So it's always a good idea to "break" the edges of all project pieces before assembling them.

Use fine abrasive paper (120-grit) on a sanding block or a fine mesh sanding pad to go over all edges. You'll still finish-sand the entire assembly prior to applying a finish.

OPTIONS TO CONSIDER
Add a plate groove

Want to display plates on the shelf? Before assembly, mount a ⅛-inch round-bottom bit in a router. With a guide attached to the router, cut a ¼-inch-deep plate groove in the top 2¼ inches in from the back edge. If you don't have a router, you can cut a shallow groove using a straight edge, backsaw, and chisel *(page 49),* **or** you could use a table saw.

Forming parts (continued)

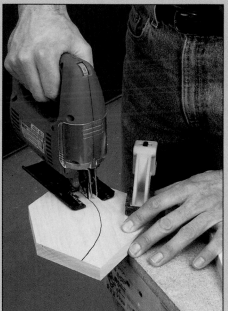

4 Make sure the side support profile aligns across the grain, as shown in the support pattern drawing *(page 65)*. Cut the straight edges. Use a jigsaw to make the curved cut along the pattern line. Repeat for second piece, then sand edges smooth.

B. Assembling the parts

1 Cut the support rail (C) to size. Refer to exploded view drawing *(page 64)* to lay out screw hole locations on the rail for mounting to wall studs (adjust for studs other than 16 inches OC). With a ⅛-inch countersink bit in an electric drill, drill holes for #8 wood screws.

2 Position support rail (C) between the two side supports (B) and check for a flush fit. Apply woodworkers glue to the ends of the support rail, position the side supports to the ends and clamp in place. Set aside and let the assembly dry.

Hanging the shelf on your wall

1 Most wood-frame homes are built with wall studs spaced 16 inches on center (OC). If you expect a shelf to support a load, you must mount it to them. Find studs with an electronic stud finder, then mark their location.

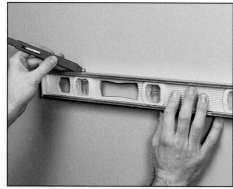

2 Use a long carpenter's level (or a smaller one on top of a straight 1×2) to draw a sight line on the wall between the marked studs. This will align with the bottom of the shelf's back support rail.

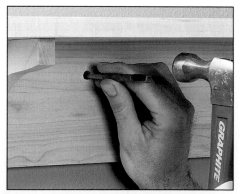

3 Have a helper assist you in lining up the shelf with the sight line, then insert a nail set through the screw holes and tap indentations in the wall. Remove the shelf and drill ⁵⁄₃₂-inch pilot holes through the wall and into the studs.

3 When assembly BC has dried, lay out and drill ⅜-inch-diameter holes ¼ inch deep from the outside of the side supports, as shown on exploded view drawing *(page 64)*. Center and drill ⁵⁄₃₂-inch pilot holes inside the ⅜-inch holes.

4 Drive #8×1½-inch flathead wood screws into screw holes in the side supports. Be sure the screws sink into the wood below the ⅜-inch holes. Then coat the holes with glue and press ⅜-inch maple mushroom head screw hole plugs into place.

5 Clamp the top and assembly BC together; all back edges should be flush. Check the assembly to mark for #8×1½-inch screws to attach the top to the supports (BC). Drill ⅜×¼-inch-deep screw holes with a centered ⁵⁄₃₂-inch pilot hole in each. Drive in the screws. Cover with plugs.

4 Reposition the shelf over the holes, then drive the #8×3-inch flathead wood screws into the shelf and wall. Complete the installation by pressing in (no glue) finished mushroom-head screw hole plugs.

WHAT IF …
You want to hide the hangers?

The simple hangers shown above, which slide over nails or screws in the wall, are less visible. Use them only if you plan to display lightweight items on the shelf; they're not strong enough for heavy loads.

COVER WITH PLUGS
Sand the plugs smooth

Mushroom-head screw hole plugs make an attractive accent, but they're an obstruction on the top. Instead, glue in ⅜-inch-diameter wood plugs, then cut them off and sand them flush with the top.

FLOATING SHELVES

With no visible means of support, these shelves appear to float on a wall. The secret is in their construction: They are built around a cleat that attaches them to the wall. The shelves' clean lines do nothing to distract from the objects placed on them. Their simple construction means you can easily make several to create an entire display wall for a collection.

Sizing for studs

The instructions here show you how to build a 24-inch shelf that spans two wall studs spaced 16 inches apart on center, but you'll have no trouble increasing the length to 36 or even 48 inches. Basic construction remains the same.

Visible options

Visit a home center and check out the variety of preshaped moldings, from contemporary to traditional, available for trim options. Almost any style will fit on the framework. Finish options are just as wide and varied, from natural to painted.

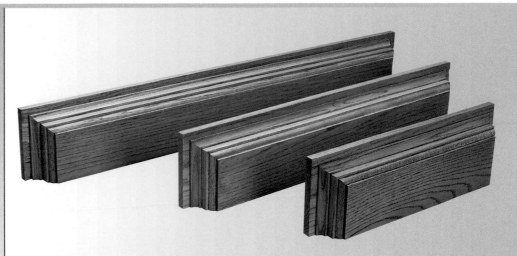

Built of red oak, these shelves employ a simple mounting cleat to give the effect of having no support at all. The same construction applies to all sizes.

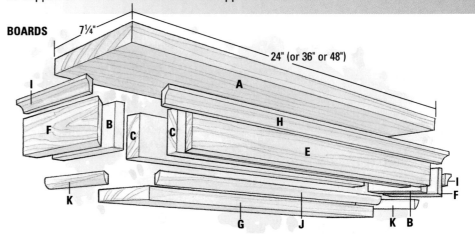

BOARDS

PRESTART CHECKLIST

☐ **TIME**
An afternoon or evening to construct, plus an hour or two for finishing

☐ **TOOLS**
Tape measure, try square, electric drill/driver, ⅛" drill bit, countersink bit, hammer, nail set, power miter saw (or miter box and backsaw), clamps, level, stud finder

☐ **SKILLS**
Sawing (making miter cuts), gluing, clamping

☐ **PREP**
Find studs at shelf location

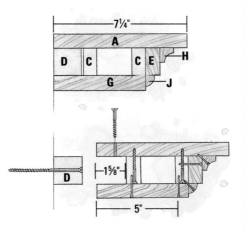

MATERIALS NEEDED

Part		Finished size			Mat.	Qty.
		T	W	L		
A	top	¾"	7¼"	24"	RO	1
B	end blocks	¾"	1½"	5"	P	2
C	front & back rails	¾"	1½"	18"	P	2
D	wall cleat	1½"	1½"	17½"	P	1
E	front rail	¾"	1½"	21"	RO	1
F	side rails	¾"	1½"	5¾"	RO	2
G	bottom	¾"	5"	19½"	RO	1
H	cove molding	¾"	¾"	22½"	RO	1
I	cove molding	¾"	¾"	6½"	RO	2
J	quarter round	½"	½"	20½"	RO	1
K	quarter round	½"	½"	5½"	RO	2

Material key: RO–red oak, P–pine
Hardware: 4d, 6d finishing nails, #16×⅝" brads, #8×1¼", ×1½", ×2", ×4" FHWS
Supplies: Glue, wood putty, sandpaper, stain, clear finish

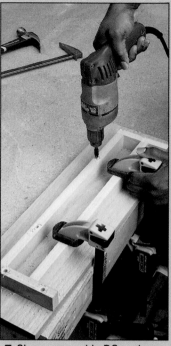

1 Crosscut the 7¼-inch-wide top (A) to 24 inches long with a miter saw. Make sure that the ends are square before proceeding.

2 Cut end blocks (B) and rails (C) to length. Position as shown, glue, and clamp. Check for square by measuring diagonally *(page 53)*; if misaligned, reposition.

3 When the glue has dried in assembly BC, drive 6d finishing nails through the end blocks and into the rails to strengthen the joints.

4 Clamp assembly BC to the underside of top (A) with end blocks flush to the back edge of the top. Secure the assembly to the top with #8×1¼-inch FHWS in countersunk holes.

ENDS ARE SQUARE
Cut once, check it twice

Clamp a layout square tightly against the board to guide a circular saw cut.

Don't take for granted that the ends of a board are square. Check each end with a try square. If you can see light between it and the board, it's not square.

COUNTERSUNK HOLES
Two-in-one bit

When instructions call for countersinking screw heads and counterboring for plugs, do them both at once with a countersink bit of proper size.

5 Dry-fit the front rail (E), which has been miter-cut at each end, and mitered side rails (F) to the front and sides of assembly BC. Glue and clamp them in place.

6 Strengthen the attachment by driving 4d finishing nails through starter holes in the front (E) and side rails (F). Sink the nailheads below the surface with a nail set, then fill the holes with wood putty.

7 Turn over the shelf assembly and apply glue to the exposed edges of parts B and C, then position the bottom (G) and clamp. Secure the bottom with 4d finishing nails and set the heads. Putty the nail holes.

ON THE WALL
Clasping a cleat

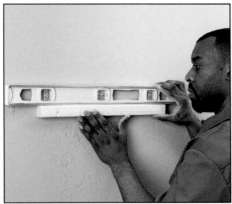

1 Use a stud sensor to locate the nearest wall studs. Position the cleat so it extends over them. Using a level, draw a pencil line on the wall at the top of the cleat. Fasten the cleat to the wall with two #8×4-inch FHWS.

2 In order to attach the shelf to the wall cleat, you'll have to drill two countersunk screw holes in the top of the shelf to accommodate #8×1½-inch FHWS.

3 Slide the shelf onto the wall cleat. Mark the screw hole locations on the cleat by inserting a finishing nail through the screw holes in the shelf and tapping lightly. Remove the shelf and drill pilot holes in the cleat.

8 From 2×2 material, cut a wall cleat (D) to length. Sand smooth all surfaces of the cleat, then insert it in the cavity at the back of the shelf to test for fit. There should be a ¼-inch gap at both ends.

9 Miter-cut cove molding (parts H and I) to size. Apply glue to the back of the cove molding pieces and clamp them in place against the bottom side of the top (A). Secure the cove molding with #16×⅝-inch brads. Set the heads and putty the holes.

10 Complete the shelf by miter-cutting the quarter-round molding (parts J and K) to size. Apply glue to the molding back and position at bottom of front rail (E) and side rails (F). Fasten with brads, set the heads, and putty the holes.

4 Reposition the shelf on the wall cleat and align it with the screw hole locations. Fasten it in place on the cleat with 1½-inch wood screws driven into countersunk holes flush with the top.

WHAT IF...
The walls are masonry?

Several types of fasteners can be used for mounting shelves to brick, concrete, or stone. Sleeve and wedge anchors expand in predrilled holes in the wall.

STANLEY PRO TIP

Drill starter holes with a nail

Driving finishing nails into hardwood moldings can be difficult. A simple, fast solution: Chuck a finishing nail of the size you're using into the drill, then use it to drill a starter hole.

MODULAR BOXES

These modular boxes, sometimes called shadow boxes, satisfy various needs, from a catch-all in the kid's room to a striking showcase for collectibles. Because they stack, you can easily move or rearrange them. Best of all, you can build seven 12×12×12-inch boxes from a single 4×8-foot sheet of plywood.

Measure before cutting

You'd think that a sheet of plywood labeled ¾ inch thick would actually be ¾ inch thick. However, that's not always the case. Because much of the plywood sold is of Asian origin (even if it's made with North American wood), it may be slightly smaller than its stated thickness. That inconsistency will throw off your measurements for the sides of these boxes, which are sawed to 10½ inches wide to allow for joining to two thicknesses of ¾-inch plywood at top and bottom (see the exploded view drawing below). So before cutting, measure the plywood's thickness, then deduct twice that from 12 inches for the width of the box sides.

Painting these birch plywood boxes and adding the distinctive ash veneer tape to the edges (bottom left) creates a first-class look. For a bright design option, completely paint the boxes (bottom right). Another option: accent the birch plywood with walnut plugs and veneer (top).

PRESTART CHECKLIST

☐ **TIME**
About four hours to build seven boxes, plus finishing time

☐ **TOOLS**
Tape measure, clamps, electric drill/driver, 1½" spade bit, ¹⁄₁₆" drill bit, table saw or portable circular saw, 40–60 tooth blade, handsaw, try square, framing square, hammer, nail set

☐ **SKILLS**
Sawing, gluing, clamping

☐ **PREP**
Assemble materials; prepare work area

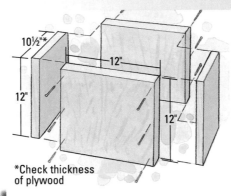

*Check thickness of plywood

MATERIALS NEEDED

Part	Finished size			Mat.	Qty.
	T	W	L		
PER BOX					
A sides	¾"	10½"	12"	BPW	2
B top/bottom	¾"	12"	12"	BPW	2

Material key: BPW–birch plywood
Hardware: 4d finishing nails
Supplies: Glue, wood putty or spackle, ash veneer tape, primer, semigloss enamel

4×8' plywood sheet

A. Cutting parts

1 To cut the tops and bottoms of the boxes, set the table saw's fence to rip 12 inches wide (or use a portable circular saw and clamped straightedge for a guide).

2 Rip two 12-inch-wide lengths from the 4×8 plywood sheet. Then rip two pieces 10½ inches wide (or according to your measurements) from the remaining stock.

3 To support plywood during crosscutting, attach an auxiliary fence of ¾-inch stock to the miter gauge with screws. Keep it about ⅛ inch from the fence to avoid binding.

4 Set the table saw blade and auxiliary fence to get a 12-inch-wide cut. Crosscut all the plywood lengths. You'll end up with fourteen 12×12-inch pieces and fourteen 10½×12-inch pieces.

SAFETY FIRST
Guard against kickback

When wood encounters a spinning saw blade, kickback can occur very quickly. On a table saw, the wood will come back at you. If you're using a portable circular saw, it's the saw that comes back.

Wood pinching the blade is the common cause of kickback. Avoid it by using a splitter in the saw kerf (the gap left by the cut) behind the blade *(page 38)* and make sure that the material you're cutting is fully supported. In addition, stay out of harm's way. At the table saw, don't stand directly in front of the blade. With a portable circular saw, don't overreach.

AUXILIARY FENCE
Check to ensure straight cuts

Square setup: To make sure that all the box pieces are square (if they're not, they won't go together properly), use a framing square to check the auxiliary fence before making a cut.

Test cut: Use some scrap plywood to make a test cut. With the framing square, check the test piece. Adjust the setup if necessary.

B. Assembling the parts

Because it's easy to go astray when assembling so many units, build a clamping jig like the one shown in Steps 1–3 to aid in the assembly process. Then use it to hold the four sides square to each other while gluing and clamping. Note: Clamping the jig in one corner, as shown in Step 3, will suffice. If one corner is square, the opposite one is also square.

Sand with caution

When finishing these modular boxes, keep in mind that hardwood plywood such as the birch plywood shown utilizes thin face veneer. If you sand too heavily in one area, it's possible to actually sand right through the veneer, an error that will telegraph through the final finish. Always maintain a light hand with abrasives, even those with fine grit. Since most plywood is fairly smooth to begin with, especially on the face side, it won't take much sanding to prepare a surface for finishing.

1 To make a clamping jig, first clamp together (no glue) a box top (B), bottom (B), and two sides (A). Be sure to assemble the pieces correctly. Measure the inside of the clamped-up box.

2 Cut scrap of ¾-inch plywood to the box's inside dimensions, minus about 1 inch on each side. With a 1½-inch spade bit in a drill, bore holes for the clamp heads about 1 inch in from two adjacent edges. These holes will accommodate the clamp heads.

Apply the finishing touches

1 Fill all plywood edges, except those at the front of the box, with spackle or wood putty.

2 Sand all filled edges smooth and lightly sand box surfaces. Remove sanding dust.

3 Apply a coat of primer to the box (except unfilled edges). Then sand lightly again.

3 Assemble the top, bottom, and two sides with glue, then clamp the box using the clamping jig to check for square. Make any necessary adjustments before the glue dries.

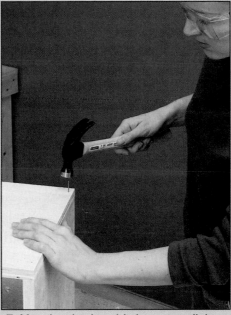

4 After the glue has dried, remove all the clamps and drive 4d finishing nails into the box's corners to reinforce the assembly. Be sure the nails enter the wood squarely. A finishing option: Use screws and plugs.

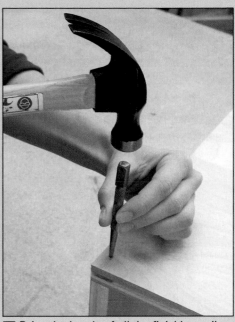

5 Drive the heads of all the finishing nails below the surface of the wood with a nail set. Fill the holes with wood putty or spackle and later sand them flush.

4 Touch up any blemishes, then paint on one or two finish coats of semigloss enamel.

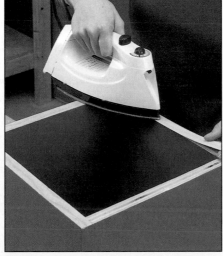

5 When the paint is dry, add ash veneer tape to the unfilled edges. Miter-cut the corners of the tape *(page 32).*

FINISHING OPTION
Use walnut plugs for accent

Join the pieces with screws in countersunk holes; plug the holes with walnut dowels for contrast. Then apply walnut instead of ash veneer tape and cover with a clear finish.

MISSION-STYLE UTILITY STAND

Shelves take the form of furniture with this Mission-style utility stand. During the Arts and Crafts Movement of the late 19th and early 20th centuries, it would have served as a library table. Nowadays it could be used as a home office printer stand, with the lower shelves providing paper and book storage.

Build it with an adjustable flat shelf, or modify it with the V-shape shelf. The drawings below show you how to modify its height, width, or depth to suit your needs. With any option, the step-by-step construction remains the same.

Material and finishing

As fitting with this style, the stand is made of oak. After staining, it is coated with clear penetrating oil. If the stand will sustain heavy use, provide tougher protection with a polyurethane finish.

PRESTART CHECKLIST

☐ **TIME**
About eight hours to construct, plus finishing time

☐ **TOOLS**
Tape measure, combination square, table saw, dado set (or backsaw), finish sander, brad-point drill bits, electric drill/driver, long bar clamps, wood chisel, dead-blow hammer

☐ **SKILLS**
Accurate measuring, sawing, and joining; chiseling

☐ **PREP**
Assemble tools and materials, prepare work area

You can change the dimensions of the piece to make it wider or deeper, for example, to hold a large-screen TV. Expand the appropriate dimension in both directions from the "cutting plane," as shown at right.

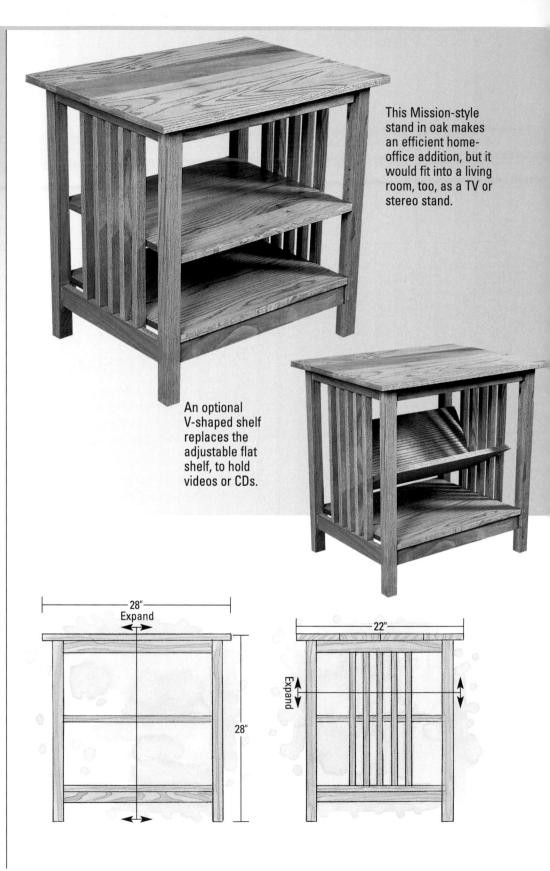

This Mission-style stand in oak makes an efficient home-office addition, but it would fit into a living room, too, as a TV or stereo stand.

An optional V-shaped shelf replaces the adjustable flat shelf, to hold videos or CDs.

28"
Expand

28"

22"

Expand

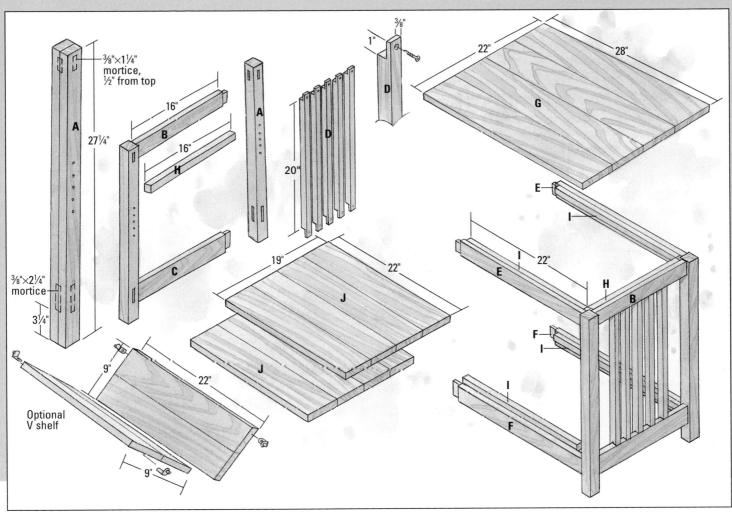

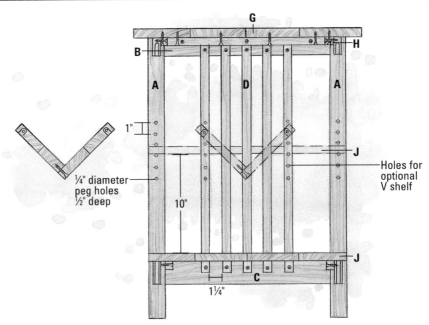

MATERIALS NEEDED

Part		Finished size			Mat.	Qty.
		T	W	L		
A	legs	1½"	1½"	27¼"	LRO	4
B	side top rail*	¾"	1¾"	18"	RO	2
C	side bottom rail*	¾"	2¼"	18"	RO	2
D	spindle	¾"	1"	22"	RO	10
E	front top rail*	¾"	1¾"	24"	RO	2
F	front bottom rail*	¾"	2¼"	24"	RO	2
G	top	¾"	22"	28"	ERO	1
H	cleats	¾"	¾"	15¼"	RO	2
I	cleats	¾"	¾"	22"	RO	4
J	bottom & shelf	¾"	19"	22"	ERO	2

Material key: RO–red oak, ERO–edge-joined red oak, LRO–laminated red oak
Hardware: #8×¾", ×1", ×1¼" FHWS, shelf pegs
Supplies: Glue, sandpaper, stain, clear oil finish
* Length includes tenons

A. Make the legs

1 Make the four legs (A) by ripping ¾-inch-thick oak into eight 1½-inch pieces. Crosscut the pieces to 27¼ inches long.

2 Glue and clamp two pieces to form a 1½×1½-inch leg. (See the Pro Tip below.) Repeat for the three remaining legs.

3 Lay out and mark ⅜×1¼-inch mortises centered on the inside surfaces at the top of the legs, ½ inch from the top (see exploded view, *page 77*). Lay out and mark the locations for ⅜×2¼-inch bottom mortises, 3¼ inch from the bottom.

Get the grain right

When gluing two pieces of wood to form a single piece (laminating), first dry-fit the pieces. Arrange them so that the grain in each piece runs in opposite directions. When glued, the leg will be stronger and more resistant to any dimensional changes due to fluctuations in humidity that may actually split the wood.

4 Chuck a ⁵⁄₁₆-inch brad-point or Forstner bit in an electric drill and bore overlapping holes to 1⅛-inch mortise depth within the layout lines.

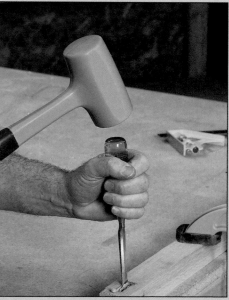

5 Use a chisel to clean out and square the mortises. Drive the chisel with a dead-blow hammer; make sure the chisel is sharp *(page 43)*.

B. Cut tenons in the rails

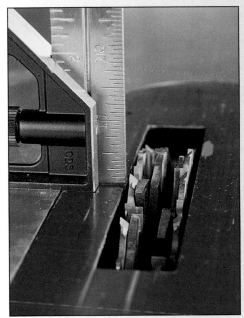

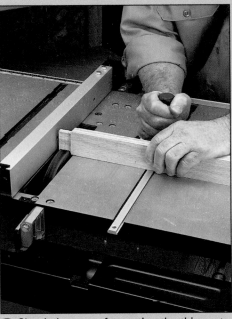

1 Rip and trim all rails (B, C, E, F) to length (finished size on *page 77* includes the length of the tenon). Install a dado set in the table saw. Adjust the blades and spacers to cut 1-inch-long tenons to fit the mortise. (The length of the tenons is ⅛ inch shorter than the depth of the mortise.)

2 Use some scrapwood to test the cut of the dado set. Cut the tenon's outside shoulders (the wider ones) first. Check its fit in the mortise. Make any necessary adjustments to the dado blades and fence. When the saw settings are correct, cut the outside shoulders on all rails.

3 Check the setup for cutting the thin part of the tenons' shoulder with a test cut on the scrapwood used in Step 2. Cut one of the rails, then check the tenon's fit in one of the mortises. If it fits, complete the tenon cuts on the rest of the rails.

WHAT IF ...
You are cutting tenons with a handsaw?

1 To cut tenons with a backsaw, first mark the cuts on the end of the piece (remember the length is ⅛ inch shorter than the depth of the mortise). Clamp the part in a bench vise and saw two of the shoulders.

2 Turn the piece and reclamp it. Saw the remaining two shoulders of the tenon. Clean up the cuts with a sharp wood chisel.

C. Add the spindles

4 Assemble two legs to a side top rail (B) and side bottom rail (C) with glue and clamp. Check for square. Repeat assembly with two more legs and side rails. When glue dries, add the front top rails (E) and front bottom rails (F) to join assemblies. Glue, clamp, check for square.

1 Before you begin making the spindles (D), verify their length by measuring between rails B and C. Allow for a 1-inch-long notch ⅝ inch deep at either end to accept the rails.

2 Set up your table saw to rip 10 spindles 1×22 inches long (or to your measurement) from ¾-inch-thick oak stock. **Use a push stick** that's narrow enough to fit between the rip fence and the saw blade.

SAFETY FIRST
Close the gaps for thin rip cuts

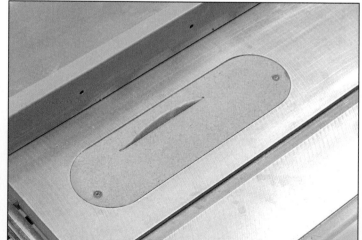

1 When ripping thin pieces (under 1 inch), make and install an auxiliary insert that keeps thin pieces out of the saw's arbor. Trace the shape of the original insert on material of the same thickness.

2 Cut out the new insert piece and install it in the arbor (with the blade all the way down). Start the blade and slowly raise it up through the piece, cutting a thin slot just big enough for the blade.

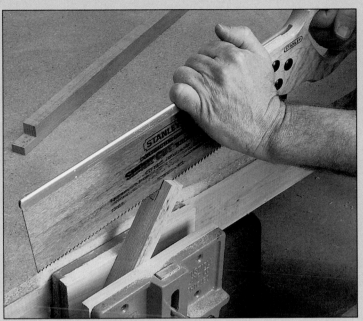

3 To cut the notches at the ends of each of the 10 spindles, refit your table saw with a dado set. Or use a backsaw to cut them, securing the wood in a bench vise and cleaning up with a sharp chisel.

4 With an electric drill and counterbore bit, drill countersunk screw holes on the back (the side away from the notch) of each spindle end, shown in the drawing on *page 77,* then attach them to the side rails.

Oversize sanding block

A standard-size sanding block that uses one-quarter of an abrasive sheet tends to leave high and low spots when smoothing long, narrow pieces or panels more than a foot square. An oversize sanding block won't do that. Tape or glue one-half of a 9×11-inch abrasive sheet to a 3×11-inch block of wood. It works in a fashion similar to a long hand plane, bridging the high and low spots across its length.

Do some finishing prep before assembly

Clean off glue squeeze-out from the joints after joining all the subassemblies. It's easier to do a thorough job now.

Sand all the spindles, too, while you can still easily get to them.

How to make up for width

Large expanses made from a single piece of wood, such as for a tabletop, will eventually crack and split due to changes in humidity. To avoid that problem, edge-join two or more narrow pieces to "make up width," as woodworkers say, for a larger piece. To create a 12-inch-wide top, for example, join three 4-inch-wide boards.

As a rule of thumb, never make up width using boards more than 6 inches wide. Narrower widths are always preferable.

The mating edges of the boards to be glued up must be true. That is, the sides have to make perfect 90-degree angles with the tops and bottoms. Check this by butting all the boards together before gluing. Then clamp them lightly to look for voids in the joints.

Clamping a wide piece from several narrower ones requires care, too. Make sure the pieces remain absolutely flat as you apply and tighten the pipe or bar clamps. Don't overtighten.

D. Add the top and shelves

1 Rip and crosscut oak to get four 5½-inch-wide by 28-inch-long pieces to build the top (G). Arrange them so the grain creates a pleasing effect, then edge-join them with glue and clamps.

2 Rip and trim cleats (H and I) to size from oak. Drill countersunk holes in the cleats for #8×1-inch FHWS, as shown in the end view drawing *(page 77)*. Attach cleats (H, I) to the inside of the top and bottom rails with screws.

(page 77)

WHAT IF ...
You'd like a V-shape shelf?

1 Rip and trim three ¾-inch-thick pieces to 4½ inches wide and 25 inches long. Cut another of the same length to 5¼ inches wide. Edge-join the 4½-inch boards, then the remaining two.

2 When the glue is dry, remove any squeeze-out, sand the wood, and join the pieces together with glue and screws in countersunk holes as shown (see *page 77*).

3 Mark peg hole locations in the spindles as shown in the V-shelf end view drawing *(page 77)*. Drill holes using a brad-point bit fitted with a stop.

(see *page 77*). ... *(page 77)*

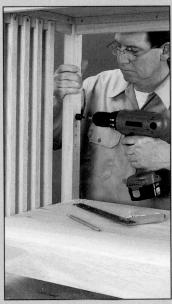

3 Drill countersunk screw holes in the undersides of cleats H and I. Position the top with an even overhang on all sides, then secure it with #8×1¼-inch FHWS through the cleats.

4 Edge-join four 4¾-inch-wide by 25-inch-long pieces for the shelf (J). Repeat for the bottom. When the glue dries, check the shelf and bottom for fit in the stand. Trim with a table saw or circular saw to fit, then sand.

5 Refer to the drawing on *page 77* for the shelf peg hole locations in the legs. Mark the holes and drill ¼-inch-diameter holes ⅜ inch deep in the legs. Use an electric drill fitted with a brad-point bit and a drill stop.

6 Insert pegs in the holes and test fit the shelf in the stand. Remove it for finishing. Test the fit of the bottom in the stand. Trim as needed, then attach to cleats with screws (or add it after finishing).

Color with stain and coat with oil

After a final sanding, use a pigmented oil or water-based stain to give the oak a warm color. Apply a penetrating oil finish. Apply at least two coats of oil. Remember—it's easier to stain and oil the shelf and the bottom before installing them in the stand.

UTILITY SHELVES

The basic design of this utility shelving unit is so versatile it can be used in a garage, large storage closet, or basement. Add as many shelves as you want between the bottom and the top; simply shorten the shelf supports for more shelves or lengthen them to create taller spaces for large items. You can easily change this unit's structural dimensions to make it deeper, longer, or higher.

Try functionally stylish

As shown, the unit uses softwood plywood and pine construction—readily available material at home centers and lumberyards. Its only finish is a coat of marine spar varnish on the shelf tops to make cleaning easier.

There's nothing stopping you, however, from painting the piece in bright-colored enamel for use in a den or playroom. In addition, the materials could be upgraded to hardwood and hardwood plywood with a clear finish for display storage.

PRESTART CHECKLIST

☐ **TIME**
About four hours

☐ **TOOLS**
Tape measure, carpenter's square, power saw, electric drill/driver, countersink bit, drill bits, level, clamps, hammer

☐ **SKILLS**
Sawing and measuring

☐ **PREP**
Assemble tools and materials, prepare a work area

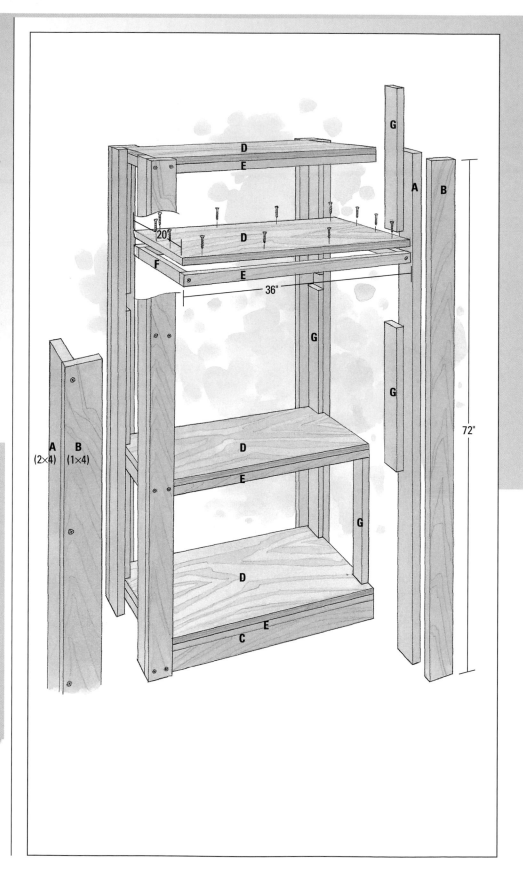

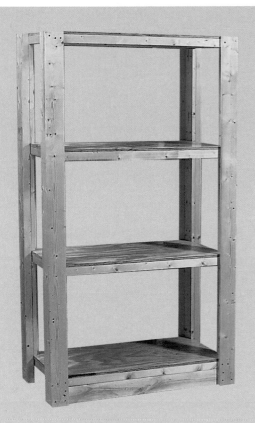

This utility shelf unit can be built quickly and easily, using low-cost materials. Its size adapts easily to fit any situation.

MATERIALS NEEDED

Part	Finished size			Mat.	Qty.
	T	W	L		
A stiles	1½"	3½"	72"	NP	4
B stiles	¾"	3½"	72"	NP	4
C base rails	1½"	3½"	36"	NP	2
D decks	¾"	20"	36"	PW	4
E front/back rails	¾"	1½"	36"	NP	8
F side rails	¾"	1½"	18½"	NP	8
G supports	¾"	3½"	*	NP	12

*As needed, see instructions.

Material key: NP–nominal pine, PW–plywood
Hardware: #8×1½", ×1¼" FHWS
Supplies: Glue, shims, sandpaper, finish

A. Forming the stiles

1 Crosscut standard 2×4 material to 72 inches in length to obtain the four stile parts (A) for the basic unit. Crosscut 1×4 material to 72 inches in length for the four stile parts (B).

2 Evenly apply glue to one edge of each 2×4 part A. Position one 1×4 part B on each part A with all ends and edges flush, then clamp and let glue dry. Clean off excess glue.

REFRESHER COURSE
Finish all sides

A finish's primary purpose is to protect the wood—from use and abuse, as well as dirt and moisture. Wood gets the most protection (especially from moisture) when all exposed sides are equally coated. With a wooden shelf, for instance, put as many coats on the bottom as you did on the top. That's especially important if the shelves will be in a harsh environment, such as a garage.

STANLEY PRO TIP

Stock off the shelf

Project plans normally include a Bill of Materials that lists the amount and sizes of all the wood parts needed. Think of this as the start of your shopping list. Rewrite it, listing the number of 1×4s, 2×4s, and other material you'll need before you go to the lumberyard or home center.

Once there, select the wood carefully. Set aside boards with obvious cosmetic defects and noticeable warp *(page 22)*. Reject boards with even slight cupping or twisting. Check by placing boards on the floor to see if they lie flat. Carry a crayon to mark the ones you're keeping.

B. Building the framework

1 Measure 2 inches in from each end of 1×4 (B) in stile assemblies. Drill five evenly spaced, countersunk holes for #8×1½-inch FHWS. Drive the screws, then sand edges.

2 Crosscut 2×4 material to 36 inches in length to make two base rails (C). Break the rail edges *(page 65)* with sandpaper.

3 Using a stop block to ensure identical length, crosscut 1×2 material to length for front and back rails (E). Repeat for eight side rails (F).

4 Clamp a straightedge as a guide and rip plywood to obtain two 36-inch-wide pieces. Crosscut the pieces to 20 inches to make four 20×36-inch shelf decks (D).

STANLEY PRO TIP

Brush on glue

Use a small foam or stiff-bristle brush to spread glue on narrow surfaces, such as the edge of a 2×4. Either squeeze ribbons of glue directly from the bottle or dip glue from a small container.

USE A STOP BLOCK
Cutting a consistent length

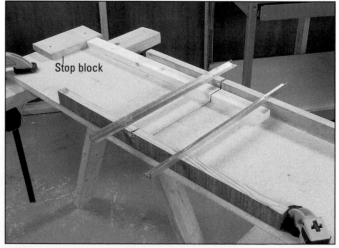

Stop block

When you have several parts to crosscut to the same length, clamp a stop block to your crosscutting jig or worktable at the desired length. Butt each board up to the stop block to make the cut.

C. Assemble shelves

1 Form a 20×36-inch base frame for each shelf by gluing and clamping two 1×2 front/back rails (E) to the ends of two 1×2 side rails (F).

2 Secure each shelf base-frame assembly by drilling holes in the front/back rails and driving #8×1½-inch FHWS into each corner of base frame.

3 Apply glue to the top of each shelf base frame (EF). Position a 20×36-inch deck (D) to the top of the shelf base frame. Check for square. Realign as needed, then clamp.

4 Mark and drill evenly spaced countersunk holes for #8×1½-inch FHWS through the deck top, into the base frame. Drive the screws to secure assemblies.

SAFETY FIRST
No chopping with a chop saw

Power miter saws, frequently called chop saws in the building trade, are accurate tools that make crosscutting and cutting at angles a snap. They cut quickly, but users have a tendency to rush the cut by pulling the blade into the wood, or "chopping," which is dangerous!

Let the blade cut the wood at its own pace. Use one hand to pull on the saw with just enough force to lower it; keep the other hand away from the blade, firmly holding the board in place against the fence.

REFRESHER COURSE
Check for square

Nothing delays a project more than having to adjust work that's out of square. So make checking for square something you do every step of the way.

Use a carpenter's square to check the ends of boards for square before and after cutting. Use a try square to check the corners of a miter joint and the ends of smaller boards, as well as for squaring a table saw blade to the table or a portable circular saw blade to the saw plate.

Diagonal measuring is one way to check for square on a four-sided assembly, such as a face frame or bookcase carcase. Use a tape measure to find the length diagonally from one corner to another. Then measure diagonally between the other two corners. If both measurements are exactly the same, the assembly is square.

D. Assemble the framework

1 Join one end of a base rail (C) to one stile assembly (AB) with a clamp. With a carpenter's framing square, check the assembly. Drill countersunk holes for two #8×1½-inch FHWS in the 1×4 face of the stile and fasten with screws

2 Add a second stile to the base rail/stile assembly and repeat Step 1. Repeat the steps to attach the two remaining stiles and the remaining base rail. Be sure to check for square at each rail/stile joint with a carpenter's framing square.

3 Position the bottom shelf on one rail/stile assembly. Drill countersunk holes for #8×1½-inch FHWS in the rail/stile through to the shelf. Then drive screws into shelf and rail/stile assembly. Add the second rail/stile assembly and fasten to shelf.

A finish to make it last

1 It may not be fine furniture, but you still want this shelving unit to feel smooth. Sand the surfaces with 120-grit abrasive, then follow with 180-grit. Soften all sharp edges too.

2 This storage unit was meant for a garage or basement, often damp places. An exterior finish such as spar varnish will protect it from moisture as well as help you keep it clean. Finish all sides.

4 With the unit lying on the floor, position the top shelf in place between the stiles, as shown in the drawing on *page 84.* Drill countersunk holes in the stiles; fasten with #8×1½-inch FHWS.

5 Cut 1×4 material for the 12 support spacers (G). To install a middle shelf, stand up the unit and clamp a support spacer to the inside of each stile. Fasten it with #8×1¼-inch FHWS in counterbored holes.

6 Slide a shelf into place on top of the support spacers. Add other shelves by repeating Step 5. You can vary the height of the middle shelves by shortening or lengthening the support spacers.

Leveling and installing the shelves

1 If the unit sits on an uneven floor, add shims to level it. Tap in shims under the stiles as needed. Check progress with a level.

2 Cut a spacer if there's a gap between the back of the top shelf and the wall. Screw through the shelf rail and the spacer, into the wall.

BOOKCASES
TO FIT YOUR HOME'S STYLE AND NEEDS

A bookcase isn't a difficult project to make, even for a novice woodworker. In its basic form, it has a framework called a carcase that includes the sides, a top, and a bottom, and a shelf or two inside. That's the simple design for the bookcase you'll learn to build on *page 92.* You can make it with nominal-size, ready-to-go lumber.

If you want more of a challenge, you can add a back to the carcase and some adjustable shelves. That's the larger bookcase described on *page 98.* It features some distinctive trim options, too, that help set it apart from the ones found at the local furniture store.

To really impress your friends, show off your woodworking skills with the built-in bookcase on *page 106.* Don't let its size or features threaten you—it's a lot easier to build than it looks! And you can customize the unit to match any decorating style.

Craft a step at a time
As with all the projects in this book, you'll have step-by-step photos to follow, plus professional tips to help you out. Study the exploded view and detail drawings, as well as the materials list, which provides dimensions for each part.

Wherever possible, the projects are broken down into subassemblies to help building move along smoothly. In this way, you'll be able to plan and divide your available construction time into manageable segments.

Practical parts
All three of the bookcases were designed with materials you'll readily find at home centers and lumberyards, including the specified moldings and hardware. Remember, however, that you always have the option of substituting other materials. For instance, you might choose walnut for the painted birch plywood in the built-in unit. Keep in mind, though, that few retail suppliers carry a full line of moldings in other than the most commonly marketed woods. Check your local stores as you plan a project.

To get exactly the piece of furniture you want, build it yourself.

CHAPTER PREVIEW

Fixed-shelf bookcase
page 92

Adjustable-shelf bookcase
page 98

Built-in bookcase
page 106

An easy way to make bookcase shelves adjustable is to install shelf rails on the sides. For a cleanly finished look, route grooves in the sides so the rails attach flush to the boards (see page 49 for more on cutting grooves).

FIXED-SHELF BOOKCASE

Sized to be built from nominal, finish-grade pine, this simple bookcase can play several roles in your home. Because it has no back and is finished on both sides, you can use it as a room divider. Add optional ready-made molding to the shelf for more of a traditional style.

If you choose to build the piece with cutout handholds on the sides, it becomes portable. The optional cutouts at the bottom give it a lighter look.

Material enlightenment

Pine, although not as strong as a hardwood like oak, withstands plenty of use and abuse. To give this bookcase the warm color of aged pine, it was first coated with orange shellac, then covered with polyurethane varnish for protection. It could be painted, if you prefer.

A less expensive but durable version could be built using medium-density fiberboard. Hardwood plywood works nicely for an upgraded look.

PRESTART CHECKLIST

☐ **TIME**
About four hours for construction, plus finishing time

☐ **TOOLS**
Tape measure, layout square, 1½" spade bit, bar and C-clamps, power saw, electric drill/driver, bits, jigsaw (optional)

☐ **SKILLS**
Measuring and sawing, clamping and gluing (routing optional)

☐ **PREP**
Assemble tools and materials, prepare work area

At 30 inches tall, this single, fixed-shelf bookcase, finished on both sides, serves as a room divider as well as an attractive and handy storage unit.

Simple design options on the sides give this case a different look and make it easily movable.

MATERIALS NEEDED

Part		Finished size*			Mat.	Qty.
		T	W	L		
A	top	¾"	13¼"	32"	EJP	1
B	sides	¾"	11¼"	30"	P	2
C	bottom	¾"	11¼"	28½"	P	1
D	shelf	¾"	11¼"	28½"	P	1
E	toe-kick rails	¾"	3½"	28½"	P	2
F	side rails	¾"	1½"	8¼"	P	2
G	apron rails	¾"	1½"	28½"	P	4
H	top cleats	¾"	1½"	9¾"	P	2

*Parts initially cut oversize, see instructions.

Material key: EJP–edge-joined pine, P–pine
Hardware: #8×1½", ×1¼" FHWS
Supplies: Glue, sandpaper, paint or clear finish

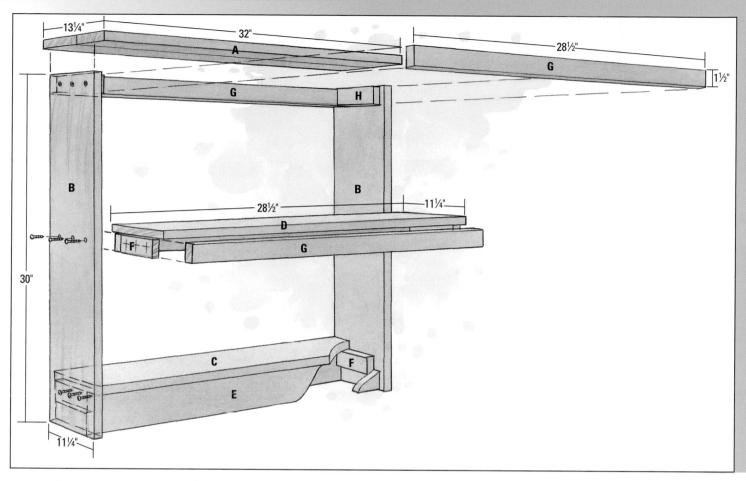

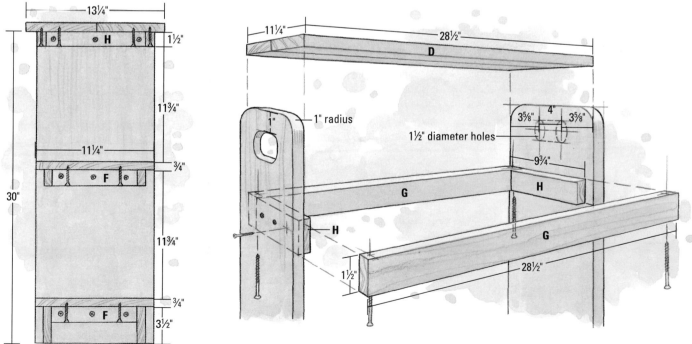

A. Cutting and preparing the parts

1 Glue and clamp two 1×8×32-inch clear pine boards to form the top (A). Set aside to dry. Then remove the glue squeeze-out from the joint lines.

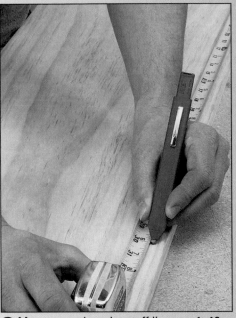

2 Measure and mark cutoff lines on 1×12 pine boards for sides (B) at 30 inches and for the bottom (C) and shelf (D) at 28½ inches. Sand all sharp edges.

3 With circular saw in a cutoff jig, or with a straightedge as a guide, crosscut the sides, bottom, and shelf to the specified lengths at marked lines.

STANLEY PRO TIP

Let wood move

Note that in this project no glue is used when fastening the framework for the top, shelf, and bottom; only screws are employed. This allows the wood to move according to humidity changes. If the frames were glued, the wood might eventually split or crack.

OPTIONS TO CONSIDER
Add handles to the sides

Want a nifty portable unit? Build this bookcase as shown in the lower photo on *page 92* and you can easily move it anywhere. For this option, extend the sides to 34 inches tall and replace the top with another shelf assembly. In other words, build two shelves of the same size.

The handhold cutouts are easy to create, as shown in the steps at right. To make the cutouts at the bottom of the sides, follow similar steps. Mark the cutouts along the bottom edge, 1½ inches from the sides.

You can rout a slight roundover on the insides of all the cutouts, as shown in Step 4. You can use sandpaper if you don't own a router.

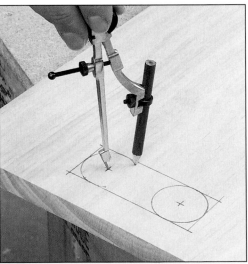

1 Draw two 1½-inch-diameter circles where shown on the optional handle drawing on *page 93*. Join them with lines to form an oval.

4 Using the setup in Step 3, mark and crosscut toe-kick rails (E) to length from 1×4 pine stock.

5 With a circular saw, crosscut the apron rails (G) and top mounting cleats (H) to length from 1×2 pine.

6 Use a table saw (or straightedge and a circular saw) to rip the top (A) to finished width of 13¼ inches. Sand all edges.

2 With a 1½-inch spade bit, drill the two holes (turn board over when halfway through and drill to finish hole).

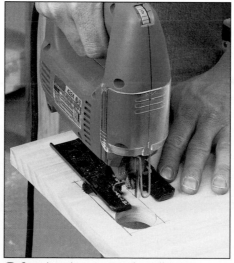

3 Complete the cutouts using a jigsaw.

4 Use a ⅛-inch roundover bit to rout the inside of the cutout.

B. Assembling the pieces

1 Glue and clamp the toe-kick rails (E) to the side rails (F) to form the framework for the bottom (C) as shown in the drawing *(page 93)*. Follow the same steps to assemble the frame for the shelf (FG).

2 Turn the bottom (C) upside down on the bench and secure the framework assembly (EF) to it with #8×1¼-inch FHWS in countersunk holes. Repeat with the frame (FG) and the shelf (D).

3 Place one side (B) on edge on the bench and position the bottom assembly on it. Clamp in place, with the toe-kick flush with the bottom of the side, and fasten with screws through the rails into the side. Repeat with the second side, supporting the first side with a piece of scrap lumber.

STANLEY PRO TIP

Use a sealer coat on pine

All pine tends to turn blotchy when stained. That's why it's always a good idea to give it a sealer coat of diluted shellac (50 percent denatured alcohol) or wood conditioner. The sealer keeps the stain from penetrating too deeply and blotching. Unthinned orange shellac gives pine the pumpkin color of aged wood. Used by itself, however, it offers little protection from spills and wear.

FINISH THE BOOKCASE
Shellac warms up the wood tone

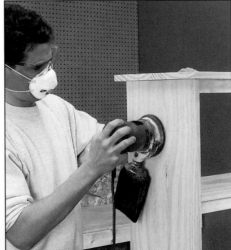

1 Sand the entire unit smooth, using progressively finer grits to 220-grit.

2 Remove sanding dust with a vacuum or tack rag, then seal with diluted orange shellac.

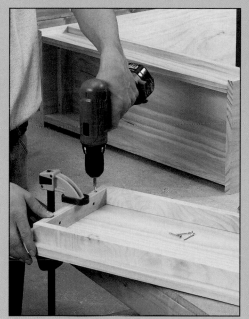

4 Glue and clamp the top cleats (H) to the apron rails (G). When the glue in the framework (GH) dries, position and secure with screws to the bottom side of the top piece (A).

5 Stand up the carcase and set the top assembly on it with the top cleats (H) fitted inside the sides, and clamp. Fasten the top with screws through the cleats into the sides. Be careful drilling, and be sure to use the proper-size screws, so they do not poke through the other side.

6 Measure between the bottom of the top frame and top of the bottom shelf. Divide this distance by two to find the location for the middle shelf. Brace the shelf with 1×2s and fasten to the sides with screws. Again, be careful drilling and use the proper-size wood screws.

3 After the shellac thoroughly dries, sand the unit lightly with #0000 steel wool to smooth the seal coat.

4 Wipe off or vacuum all sanding dust and apply a finish coat or two of polyurethane varnish to all surfaces.

ADJUSTABLE-SHELF BOOKCASE

This bookcase features two adjustable shelves. Its double-wall construction adds strength to the unit while concealing the plywood edges, and creates flush sides that allow you to slide out books without them catching on the face frame. The design is easily expandable in height, and its subassembly construction comes together so quickly that you may want to build two of them at the same time to flank a window or fireplace.

Other materials

Red oak plywood is the material of choice here, but you can save money by using melamine-coated fiberboard and concealing the edges with veneer tape. Painted birch plywood is another practical option, and it's stronger than fiberboard. Built as shown, the bookcase makes an impressive addition to your home's den or living room.

Three feet wide and 4 feet tall, this adjustable-shelf oak bookcase holds dozens of tomes, or displays your treasures.

To add more visual interest to the design, cut this shape into the front base. The cutout is made 5 inches from each end, ½ inch deep, with a ½-inch-radius corner.

PRESTART CHECKLIST

☐ **TIME**
About eight hours to build, plus finishing time

☐ **TOOLS**
Tape measure, try square, framing square, electric drill/driver, bits, countersink bit, table saw, bar clamps, router, router bits, hammer, nail set

☐ **SKILLS**
Measuring, sawing

☐ **PREP**
Assemble materials and tools, prepare large work area

MATERIALS NEEDED

Part		Finished size*			Mat.	Qty.	Part		Finished size*			Mat.	Qty.
		T	W	L					T	W	L		
A	sides	¾"	11"	42¼"	RPWD	2	I	front base	¾"	3½"	36"	RO	1
B	top/bottom	¾"	11"	33"	RPWD	2	J	side base	¾"	3½"	12¾"	RO	2
C	base rail	¾"	3½"	33"	Any	1	K	top panel	¾"	12"	34½"	RPWD	1
D	end rails	¾"	3½"	10½"	Any	2	L	front edging	¾"	1½"	36"	RO	1
E	side panels	¾"	11¼"	47¼"	RPWD	2	M	side edges	¾"	1½"	12¾"	RO	2
F	stiles	¾"	1½"	47¼"	RO	2	N	back	¼"	33"	43¾"	RPWD	1
G	top rail	¾"	1½"	31½"	RO	1	O	shelves	¾"	11"	31½"	RPWD	2
H	bottom rail	¾"	4½"	31½"	RO	1	P	edging	¾"	1½"	31½"	RO	2

Material key: RO–red oak, RPWD–red oak plywood, Any–poplar, pine, etc.
Hardware: #8×1½", ×1¼" FHWS, #6×1" FHWS, 1" brads (optional)
Supplies: wood putty, sandpaper, finish

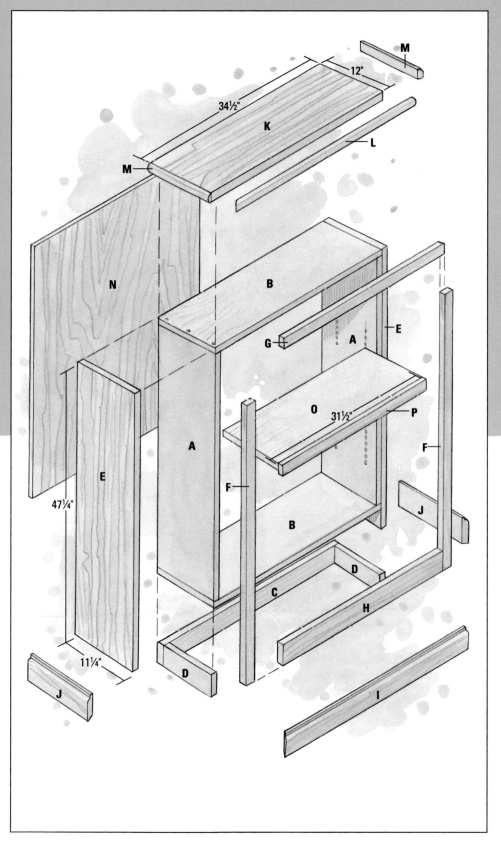

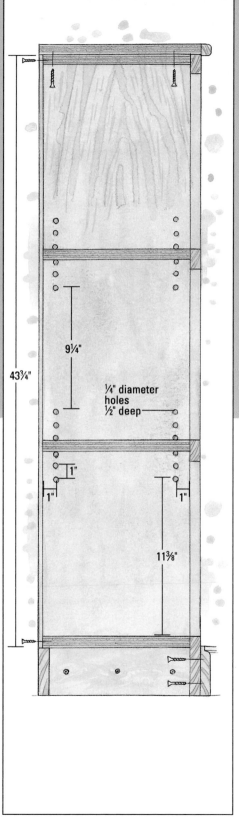

A. Drill shelf-pin holes

1 Cut and trim the sides (A) to size. Clamp a scrap of perforated hardboard (pegboard) to the sides as a template to lay out and mark locations for shelf-pin holes as shown in the exploded view drawing *(page 99)*.

2 With sides on a bench, drill ¼-inch holes ⅜ inch deep at shelf-pin hole locations. Use an electric drill fitted with a brad point bit and a drill stop. Check the depth frequently; do not overdrill.

B. Join the inner carcase

1 Cut the top (B) to size. Join it to the end of one side (A) with glue and #8×1½-inch FHWS in counterbored holes, with parts lying on the table as shown. Add the second side.

REFRESHER COURSE
Support plywood for ripping

To safely rip plywood with a portable circular saw, use 2×4 supports resting on sawhorses and a kerf splitter to prevent kickback.

STANLEY PRO TIP

No drill stop? Try tape.

You can control the depth of the holes you drill without a drill stop by wrapping tape around the bit as a visible guide to the proper depth.

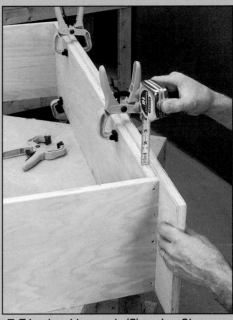

2 Cut the bottom (B) to size. With the sides/top assembly in place, clamp and glue the bottom to the sides. Check for square by measuring diagonally. Fasten with #8×1½-inch FHWS.

3 Rip and trim the base rail (C) and the end rails (D) to size. On a table, join the base rail to end rails with glue. Secure with #8×1½-inch FHWS in counterbored holes.

4 Trim the side panels (E) to size. Glue and clamp one panel to the side (A) of carcase with the front edges flush. Glue and clamp the second side panel to the other side. Let the glue dry, then glue and clamp the base/end rails (CD) in place.

OPTIONS TO CONSIDER
Make your own molding

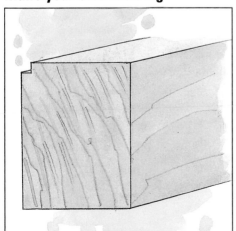

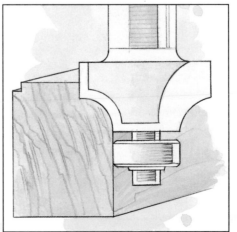

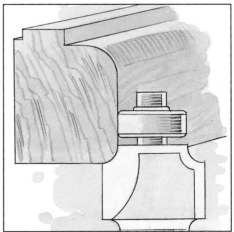

1 To profile the top molding, rip ¾-inch oak to 1 inch wide. Use a table saw or router to cut a ¹⁄₁₆×¹⁄₁₆-inch rabbet on one edge.

2 With a roundover bit in a router, shape a ¼-inch roundover ⅛ inch deep on the edge opposite the rabbet.

3 To complete the molding profile, chuck a ⅛-inch roundover bit into the router and shape a ⅛-inch roundover along the bottom edge.

C. Stick-build the face frame

1 Cut the stiles (F) and the top and bottom rails (G, H) of the face frame to size. Glue and clamp one stile to the face of the carcase and flush with the side. Dry-fit the other stile and the two rails to the clamped stile to check for fit. Trim as needed for a tight butt joint.

2 Glue and clamp the top and bottom rails to the carcase face flush with its sides and butted to the first stile. Dry-fit the second stile to check for fit. Trim as necessary, then glue and clamp in place to complete the face frame assembly.

3 Rip and crosscut the front base (I) and the side bases (J) to size. Cut a rounded edge on the top edges using a ⅜-inch bit in a router. Measure and miter-cut both ends of the front base and one end of each side base. Glue and clamp in place on the carcase. Sand the subassembly.

REFRESHER COURSE
Dowel-jointed frame

Another way to build the face frame is to construct it as a separate assembly. Use dowel joints *(page 47)* to secure the stiles to the rails, then glue and clamp the frame to the carcase.

SAND THE SUBASSEMBLY
Make finishing easier

It may be difficult to finish-sand some parts of a project after assembly, such as the bookcase face frame, because you can't get into the corners and other tight places. Sanding a subassembly before adding it to the project ensures a thorough finishing job.

D. Make and install the top

1 Cut the plywood top (K) to size. Position it on the bookcase carcase, clamp, and fasten it in place with #8×1¼-inch FHWS in counterbored holes from the inside. Drill carefully; don't go through the top. Be sure to use the right size screws.

2 From a length of red oak, rip and crosscut the front edging (L) and the side edgings (M). Measure and miter-cut both ends of the front edging to length, then glue and clamp it to the front edge of the top.

3 With the front edging in place, double-check the mitered lengths for the side edgings. Miter-cut one end of each and dry-fit to the top. Glue and clamp the side edgings in place.

CONSIDER THE OPTIONS
Trim with cove molding

The design options for this bookcase include a top made of edge-joined solid oak. Round over top edges with a router and roundover bit, then add a piece of ¾-inch oak cove molding beneath it.

Top edge options

You can give the bookcase top a more finished look without adding edge molding by routing its top and bottom with a ⅛-inch roundover bit (top). Rout the piece on a router table before it's attached or by working with a hand-held router after it is on the case.

Another option is to add a profiled molding to the top edge. See the step-by-step instructions on *page 101* to make your own.

E. Complete the basic assembly

1 Attaching the finish sides to the carcase created a rabbeted frame for the bookcase back. Measure inside that frame to get the final dimensions for the back (N).

2 From ¼-inch-thick red oak plywood, cut the back panel. Lay the bookcase face down on sawhorses and insert the back (N) to check its fit. Trim as necessary.

3 With the back in place, mark it for regularly spaced screw holes along its edges. Drill holes for short #6×1-inch FHWS. Then remove the back for now.

REFRESHER COURSE
Cut the right side

All plywood has a good side and a not-so-good side. When working with expensive hardwood plywood, keep in mind which is the best or "face" side, because a saw blade leaves rough edges on the side from which it exits the wood.

 If you cut plywood with a portable circular saw, position the sheet with the face toward the floor. The saw blade turns counterclockwise (as you attach the blade), thus exiting on the not-so-good side. With a table saw, it's just the opposite: The blade turns clockwise and exits the bottom. In this case, saw with the best side of the plywood up *(page 39)*.

REMOVE THE BACK
Finishing the back requires extra attention

Trying to finish the back while it's attached to the bookcase results in uneven application, simply because it's hard to reach all of it. After fitting the back and drilling screw holes, remove it for sanding, staining, and finishing in a well-lit work area. When the back is dry, reinstall it in the bookcase and secure it with small wood screws. You may want to finish it on both sides for complete protection.

4 Cut the shelves' edging (P) to size from red oak, and shape the edging as desired. Cut two shelves from plywood, then glue and clamp the edging to the front of them.

5 Install the shelf support pins in the drilled holes at desired shelf height. Then temporarily install the shelves to check for fit. Trim the shelves as necessary, then sand.

6 Sand, stain, and apply a finish to the bookcase, shelves, and back. When the finish has cured, reinstall the back panel and secure it with screws.

SHAPE THE EDGING
Shelf edge options

Adding a solid wood edge to the red oak plywood shelves covers the unsightly plies and adds rigidity. A simple 1½-inch-wide strip ripped from ¾-inch-thick red oak will do (top). But an attractive option is to rout ⅛-inch roundovers on the 1½-inch strip (bottom). Cutting a 1/16×1/16-inch rabbet at the strip's back imparts another detail.

SAND, STAIN, AND FINISH
Plywood requires a light touch

1 Modern hardwood plywood uses extremely thin face veneers. When sanding, make one pass with 180-grit sandpaper, a second with 220-grit. That's all you'll need before staining.

2 Apply stain and let it dry. We used a penetrating oil for a top coat, with two applications. Sand with fine abrasive or #0000 steel wool between coats for ultra smoothness.

BUILT-IN BOOKCASE

Although the term *built-in* has an air of permanence about it, this bookcase doesn't require remodeling a wall to accommodate it. Creating a built-in look isn't complicated; the unit's construction follows the same approach used for previous projects: building subassemblies first, then joining them, as with the adjustable-shelf bookcase project on the preceding pages. You can trim this design with ready-made moldings selected to match your decorating scheme and furniture style.

Appearance options

To achieve a colonial look, the unit shown here was built of birch hardwood plywood because the material readily accepts paint. Paintable moldings are available in the same style. You can just as easily construct the bookshelf of red oak or cherry plywood. Find out what materials are available locally and decide what best fits your budget and taste.

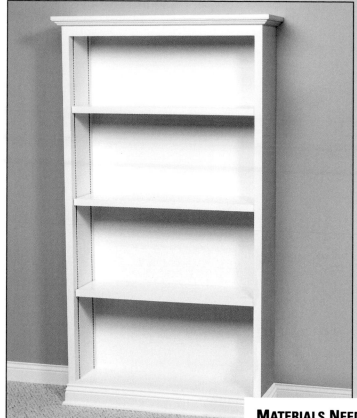

At more than 6 feet tall by 3 feet wide, this unit is an imposing piece that commands a wall and demands attention in a living room, dinning room, or den.

PRESTART CHECKLIST

☐ **TIME**
About 16 hours to construct

☐ **TOOLS**
Tape measure, try square, carpenter's square, table saw, miter saw or miter box and backsaw, coping saw, router, router bits, drill/driver and bits, countersink bit, dowel pins, bar/pipe clamps, hammer, nail set, finish sander

☐ **SKILLS**
Measuring, sawing, drilling

☐ **PREP**
Assemble tools and materials; prepare a large work area

To conceal storable items, it's easy to add hinged doors to this bookcase unit when building it or even at a later date. The doors close against the lower shelf.

MATERIALS NEEDED

Part	Finished size			Mat.	Qty.
	T	W	L		
A stiles	¾"	1½"	76"	PL	2
B top rail	¾"	3"	36"	PL	1
C bottom rail	¾"	4¾"	36"	PL	1
D sides	¾"	11¼"	72"	BPW	2
E top/bottom	¾"	11¼"	36"	BPW	2
F finished sides	¾"	12"	76"	BPW	2
G top	¾"	13½"	40½"	BPW	1
H edging*	¾"	¾"	72"	PL	
I back	¼"	36"	72"	BPW	1
J shelves	¾"	10½"	36"	BPW	3
K shelf edging	¾"	1¼"	36"	PL	3
READY-MADE MOLDINGS:					
L colonial base	½"	4¼"	8'		
M quarter round	½"	¾"	8'		
N bed rail (or cove)	1⅛"	1½"	8'		

*Cut for three pieces, see instructions.

Material key: PL–poplar, BPW–birch plywood
Hardware: #8×1½", ×1¼" FHWS, #6×¾" FHWS, 4d and 6d finishing nails, shelf standards, shelf supports, wraparound hinges (optional), door pulls (optional), magnetic catch (optional)
Supplies: Glue, ⅜" dowel pins, putty or spackle, sandpaper, primer, paint

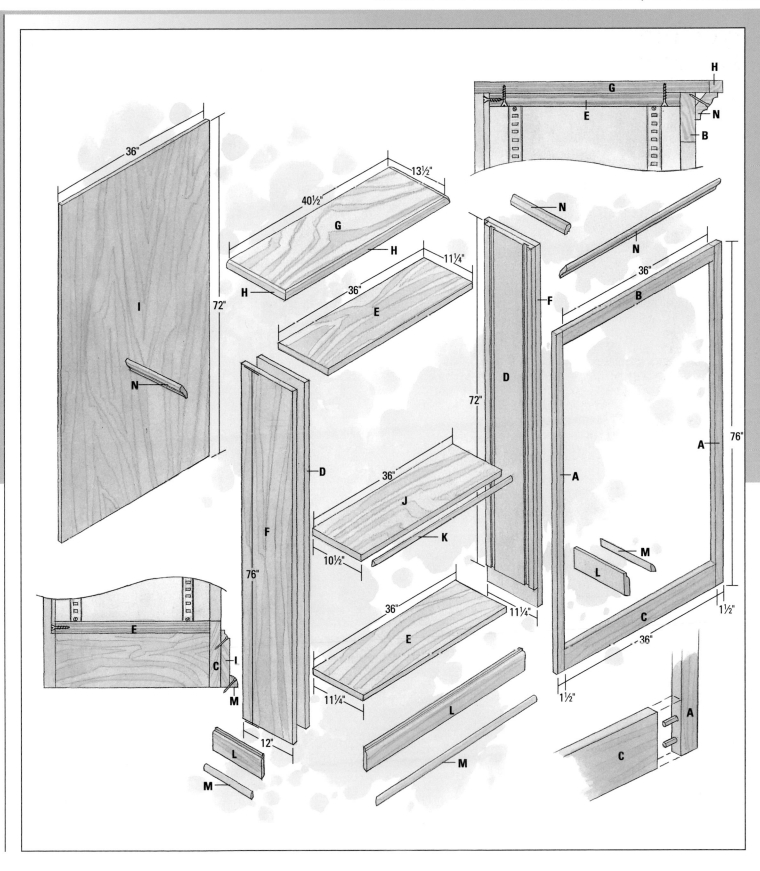

A. Building the face frame

1 Rip and trim face frame stiles (A) and top and bottom rails (B, C) from solid stock. Refer to the exploded view and dowel joint detail drawings *(page 107)* to mark the dowel locations. Drill holes in parts A, B, and C where shown and insert the dowels.

2 Glue the dowel joints and assemble the face frame. Use bar clamps to hold the assembly. Before the glue dries, check the frame assembly for square by measuring diagonally. Loosen the clamps, adjust as necessary, then retighten clamps.

3 When the glue has dried, remove the clamps. Scrape off excess glue with a chisel or putty knife. Sand the face frame surfaces smooth with a finish sander or sandpaper and sanding block. Set the assembly aside.

CONSIDER THE OPTIONS
Add some doors

1 To build doors, rip and crosscut plywood to get two ¾×17¾×17¾-inch panels.

2 Add paintable veneer tape to their exposed edges (or fill and sand).

B. Building the carcase

1 From ¾-inch birch plywood, rip the two sides (D) and the top and bottom (E) to 11¼ inches wide. Then crosscut the sides, top, and bottom to length as specified in the Materials Needed box on *page 106*.

2 Measure all four of the shelf standards you've chosen to get their exact width and thickness (they can vary by manufacturer). Later, you might have to trim them to exact length with a hacksaw.

3 On the inside of the sides (D), lay out and mark locations for the shelf-standard grooves 1¼ inch from each edge and along the length of the sides (see exploded view drawing on *page 107)*. Double-check locations.

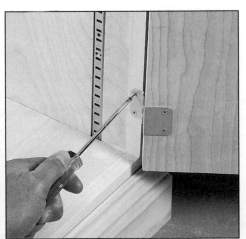

3 Fasten a pair of wraparound hinges to each door. After finishing, mark the locations of pull knobs and latches, and drill holes.

4 Install a shelf to the case. Dry-fit the doors in the opening to find and mark hinge screw hole locations on the face frame. Pre-drill the screw holes. Mark locations for latches.

5 To hang the doors, support them with wood blocks and screw on the hinges. After fitting the hardware, remove it and the doors for finishing. Reassemble after finishing.

Building the carcase (continued)

4 Clamp a long straightedge to the sides (or use a router guide) to cut along the groove marks. Chuck a ⅝-inch (or your measure) straight cutting bit in a router and set its depth to the standard's thickness. Then rout the grooves.

5 Lay the sides and top and bottom on the floor or workbench, apply glue to the ends of top and bottom (E), and glue and clamp to the insides of sides (D). Check the assembly for square with diagonal measure.

6 Remove clamps from the assembly and drill countersunk holes in the sides where they join with the top and bottom. With a drill/driver, secure the joints with #8×1½-inch FHWS.

7 Rip and crosscut to specified size the finished ends (F), top (G), and shelves (J) from ¾-inch birch plywood. Then set the top and shelves aside until needed.

8 Apply glue to the inside of one finished end (F) and position it to side (D). End of F must fit flush with D at the front and top. Add the second finished end to the other side; glue, position, then clamp all in place.

9 Dry-fit the face frame to the front of the carcase with top and sides flush. Adjust as necessary; apply glue to carcase edges and clamp face frame in place until the glue dries. Remove all glue squeeze-out.

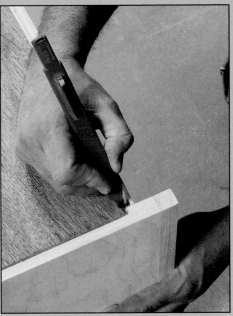

10 Measure the area inside the rabbet formed at the back of the case. Cut the back panel (I) to those dimensions from ¼-inch-thick plywood and dry-fit in case.

11 If the fit is too tight or slightly off, mark the areas that need trimming and recut or sand to remove excess.

12 Once satisfied with the fit, fasten it in place by driving #6×¾-inch woodscrews around the perimeter. If desired, you can later remove it for finishing.

Add the base trim

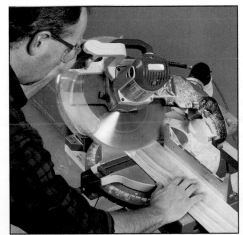

1 Buy an 8-foot length of colonial base molding 4¼ inches wide (or buy a molding style to match the existing molding on the wall). Measure for the front piece and miter-cut the ends.

2 Glue and nail the front piece in place. Measure and cut the side moldings; miter one end of each. Leave the other ends square for a freestanding case. For a built-in look, see *pages 114–115*.

3 Dry-fit the side moldings and check the fit of the mitered joints. Attach the side moldings to the case with glue and 4d finishing nails. Sink the nailheads below the surface with a nail set.

C. Adding the top

1 From ¾-inch-thick stock, rip a 72-inch strip ¾ inch wide for top edging (H). Crosscut the strip to obtain two 14¼-inch-long pieces and one 42 inches long. Miter-cut the ends of the long piece and one end of each side piece. Glue to top (G).

2 When glue has dried, clean off any glue squeeze-out with a chisel or putty knife, then use a finish sander to sand the edging flush with the top. Sand the top and bottom edges of edging to obtain a rounded edge.

3 Position the top on the bookcase with an even overhang at the front and sides, then clamp in place. Mark and drill evenly spaced countersunk screw holes for #8×1¼-inch FHWS in the top of the case from inside. Screw the top to the carcase.

4 Miter-cut both ends of a piece of bed rail molding to fit under the front of the edged top (42 inches, but measure to be sure). Apply glue to the back edges of the molding, position it under the top, and secure it in place with 4d finishing nails. Sink the nailheads.

5 Measure the sides of the case from back to the mitered front molding and cut two shorter pieces of bed rail molding to fit. Miter only one end of each piece to join with the front molding. Dry-fit to check its length, then glue and nail in place.

STANLEY PRO TIP

Avoid glue splotches

When edge-joining boards to make a top, you want to see glue squeeze-out to indicate that you've used enough adhesive to cover the joint. But glue splotches can botch up your finishing efforts, and glue on your hands can cause them. Have both a damp and a dry cloth nearby as you work. Wipe your hands first with the damp cloth, then quickly dry them with the other so you won't dampen the wood.

D. Building the shelves

1 Rip and crosscut the shelves (J). Trim the shelf edging (K) to size. For shelf edge options, see *pages 33, 105.* For a cleaner, more finished look, cut shelf-pin recesses in the bottom of the shelves.

2 Glue and clamp the shelf edging in place. Sand and paint.

3 Dry-fit and trim the shelf standards as needed. Rather than masking off the shelf standards, install them after you've finished the bookcase. Set them aside until the finishing is done.

SHELF-PIN RECESSES
Make a jig for the router

Measure and mark the shelf-pin recesses on the bottom of the shelves. With a straight-cutting bit in a handheld router, rout the recesses in the shelves. A jig made from scrap pieces limits router travel and simplifies repetitive cuts.

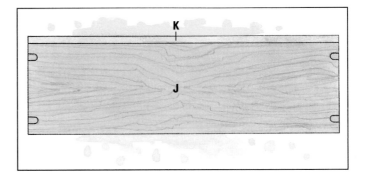

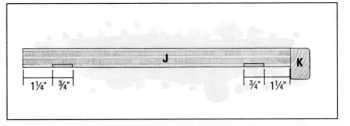

1¼" ¾" ¾" 1¼"

E. Finishing the pieces

1 When you're planning to paint, it's OK to skip the extra-fine grits needed to sand wood that will receive a clear finish. Sand first with 120-grit, then finish with 180-grit. Even if you use an electric sander, keep a sanding block on hand for corners and crevices.

2 Details, such as the curves and troughs in moldings, are best sanded with fine mesh sanding pads that easily fit the contours. Be sure to vacuum or use a tack cloth to wipe off all sanding dust.

3 A coat of primer allows you to spot and correct any slight imperfections you may not have noticed when sanding. Primer also provides a good base for the finish coat.

STANLEY PRO TIP

Speed up painting time

A bookcase with several removable shelves usually means double the painting time as you wait for one freshly finished side to dry before turning it over to coat the second side.

To speed things up and avoid the need for touch-up painting as well, drive ¾-inch brads through some pieces of ½-inch-thick scrapwood. After you've coated one side of a shelf, pick it up by the ends and place it on several of these homemade holders to keep the painted side off the work surface while you coat the second side. You'll never notice the tiny pin pricks left in the paint by the brads' sharp points. But if you do, you can quickly coat them when the entire shelf is dry.

ACHIEVING A BUILT-IN LOOK
Cutting a profiled molding

1 To make room for the bookcase, cut out and remove a section of the wall's base molding as wide as the bookcase.

2 Miter-cut the bookcase's side base molding at the wall end. Pencil on the profile of the wall molding, then cut the molding to the profile with a coping saw.

F. Completing the assembly

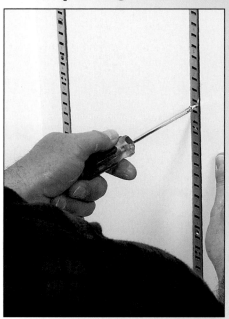

4 Brush on (or spray) semigloss enamel, carefully avoiding runs on vertical surfaces. Complete coverage of the wood, and a smooth final finish, usually requires two coats.

Install the shelf standards. Unless you want to mask off the standards before painting, it saves time and labor to hold off installing them until after the unit has been finished.

Attach the shoe molding after the unit is in place against the wall. If there are any slight gaps between the bookcase and the floor, the molding will hide them.

3 Position the bookcase back against the wall. Fit the coped molding end against the wall molding; mark the length of the piece to join the front base molding. Miter-cut the side molding to fit.

SAFETY FIRST
Fasten the bookcase to the wall

1 Because of this unit's height, you may want to secure it to the wall with #10×3-inch roundhead woodscrews (RHWS). Locate the studs in the wall behind where you'll place the unit (one is OK, two is better). Mark the screw locations on the upper back of the cabinet to coincide with stud locations.

2 Drill holes in the back and in the wall for the screws. Position the cabinet against the wall and drive screws into the wall studs.

GLOSSARY

Air-dry: Describes sawn lumber that has not been artificially seasoned; a moisture content of about 12 percent.

Arbor: A rotating metal shaft on a woodworking machine to which another rotating part, usually a bit or blade, is attached.

Banding: Solid wood trim attached to plywood edges to conceal plies.

Bevel: An angle of less than 45 degrees shaped on the edge of wood.

Biscuit joint: A joint that uses wooden wafers glued into slots cut in edges of mating pieces.

Board foot: The volume measurement of hardwood lumber, calculated by multiplying length times width times thickness and dividing by 144 cubic inches.

Bore: To drill a large hole.

Bow: A warp in which the ends of a board both curve in a direction away from the desired plane, normally the length.

Brad-point: A type of drill bit with two cutting edges and a guiding centerpoint.

Break: The action of sanding wood edges to remove sharpness.

Burl: The swirling figure in wood grain caused by growths on the outside of the tree or root.

Carcase: The box-like component of a cabinet that surrounds and encloses its doors, drawers, or shelves.

Chamfer: The edge of a board that has been beveled at a slight angle.

Check: A drying defect evidenced by small splits in the ends of a board.

Collet: A device that positions and secures a bit to the shaft in a router.

Counterbore: A screw hole deep enough to accept a wooden plug after the screw is in place.

Countersink: A drilled hole that fits the shape of a wood screw.

Crosscut: A cut across grain that reduces material to a desired length.

Cutter: A sharp cutting edge.

Dado (groove): A channel cut in wood that runs across the grain. A groove is a channel that runs with the grain.

Dowel: A small-diameter, round piece of wood.

Dry-fit: Preliminary joining of wood assemblies without glue to check fit.

Edge grain: The edge of a board that was flat (plain) sawn perpendicular to the growth rings.

End grain: The porous wood at the ends of a board.

Face frame: A four-piece wooden assembly attached to the front of a cabinet.

Face grain: The pattern of the grain on the largest surface of a board.

Featherboard: A kerfed safety device, usually of wood, that holds a board securely against a table saw or router table fence.

Feed: The action of moving wood into a machine, such as a table saw.

Figure: The visible arrangement of wood grain in a pattern.

FHWS: Abbreviation for flat-head woodscrew.

Forstner bit: A patented bit for drilling holes that do not fully penetrate the wood and leave a flat-bottomed hole.

Frame-and-panel: Construction that employs a wooden frame to enclose an unattached flat wooden panel.

Grain direction: The direction in which the dominating, elongated fibers lie in a piece of sawn wood.

Green: Describes wood that still contains most of the moisture it had while part of the tree.

Heartwood: The usually darker, mature wood at a tree's center.

Hone: To refine and polish a cutting edge against a hard, slightly abrasive surface or material.

Jig: A specialty device that holds a workpiece or tool in a certain way to efficiently and accurately perform a sawing or shaping operation.

Joining: Permanently fastening one piece of wood to another.

Jointing: The technique of using a machine (jointer) or hand plane to create two surfaces perfectly perpendicular to each other, such as the edge of a board to its face.

Kerf: The slot left by a saw blade as it cuts through material.

Kiln-dry: Describes artificially seasoned wood with a moisture content of 6-9 percent.

Make-up: Joining smaller pieces of wood to obtain ones that are wider (typical) or longer.

Miter: A 45-degree angle cut on a piece of wood.

Moisture content: The percentage, by weight, of moisture in wood at any given time.

Molding: Shaped wood used as trim.

Mortise: An opening cut in a piece of wood to accept a mating piece of wood (tenon).

Nominal: The generic dimension of sawn lumber, e.g. 2×4, which actually measures less, 1½×3½ inches.

Open time: The time interval between when adhesive is applied and when it can no longer be worked; also called working time.

Outfeed: The exit of wood from a machine, such as a table saw.

Pilot: A guide, such as on a router bit.

Pilot hole: A hole drilled to guide a screw into wood.

Plunge cut: Starting a saw in wood away from an edge.

Pocket-hole: A joining technique that employs screws driven at an angle.

Pushstick: A safety device used to feed wood into a saw blade.

Rabbet: A channel sawn or formed on the edge of a board or panel.

Rail: One of the two horizontal pieces in a face frame.

Resaw: To saw a thick board into thinner ones without reducing length or width.

RHWS: Abbreviation for round-head woodscrew.

Rip: To reduce a wide board or sheet goods in width by sawing lengthwise.

Rout: Shaping or cutting wood with a router.

Sapwood: The outermost wood in the trunk of a tree; the usually lighter-colored wood in a board.

Slot cutter: A router bit designed to cut a slot in the edge of a board.

Square: A measuring device used to detect the accuracy of wood pieces joined at 90 degrees; the alignment of wood joined at 90 degrees.

Squeeze-out: The thin ribbon of glue forced out of a clamped joint.

Stile: One of the two vertical pieces in a face frame.

Stop block: A piece of wood clamped in place to limit the sawn length of a board.

Stopped cut: A channel (dado, groove, or rabbet) that does not exit the wood.

Straightedge: A metal or wood implement clamped to the workpiece to ensure a straight cut.

Tenon: The tongue-like extension cut on the end of a piece of wood to fit into a mating mortise.

Toe-kick: The wood part that is recessed beneath a cabinet base.

Veneer: Very thin sheets or strips of solid wood.

Warp: The misshapen form(s) that a board sometimes acquires in drying after sawn from a log.

Waste: Solid wood and residue left after wood has been cut or machined.

Workpiece: A board or piece of wood in the process of being machined.

INDEX

METRIC CONVERSIONS

U.S. Units to Metric Equivalents			Metric Units to U.S. Equivalents		
To convert from	Multiply by	To get	To convert from	Multiply by	To get
Inches	25.4	Millimeters	Millimeters	0.0394	Inches
Inches	2.54	Centimeters	Centimeters	0.3937	Inches
Feet	30.48	Centimeters	Centimeters	0.0328	Feet
Feet	0.3048	Meters	Meters	3.2808	Feet
Yards	0.9144	Meters	Meters	1.0936	Yards
Square inches	6.4516	Square centimeters	Square centimeters	0.1550	Square inches
Square feet	0.0929	Square meters	Square meters	10.764	Square feet
Square yards	0.8361	Square meters	Square meters	1.1960	Square yards
Acres	0.4047	Hectares	Hectares	2.4711	Acres
Cubic inches	16.387	Cubic centimeters	Cubic centimeters	0.0610	Cubic inches
Cubic feet	0.0283	Cubic meters	Cubic meters	35.315	Cubic feet
Cubic feet	28.316	Liters	Liters	0.0353	Cubic feet
Cubic yards	0.7646	Cubic meters	Cubic meters	1.308	Cubic yards
Cubic yards	764.55	Liters	Liters	0.0013	Cubic yards

To convert from degrees Fahrenheit (F) to degrees Celsius (C), first subtract 32, then multiply by $\frac{5}{9}$.

To convert from degrees Celsius to degrees Fahrenheit, multiply by $\frac{9}{5}$, then add 32.